What people say

This is an excellent guide for patients, and those using computers as part of their general life styles.

**Simon Griffiths
Registered Osteopath, Kent and Hampshire**

Your book to be part o, start-up pack for everyone using computers.

**Dr Joe Olliver,
St Cross College,
Oxford University**

I was shocked when I read your book. I realised we were doing nothing right for the children! We reviewed working conditions of all computers and took action.

**Elsa Christie,
(Former)
Head Teacher,
Unicorn School
for the Dyslexic
Child, Abingdon**

With RSI I could not do my job, play the piano, or do many everyday things. But by following the advice in this book I rarely have symptoms.

**Jill Ewbank,
Architect**

*Today I had a patient with awful symptoms after only two months of mousing.
I mentioned your book. I think the demand would be significant.*

**Dr Andy Chivers
GP, Oxford**

Your book is well put together and very readable. It would be great if it were in every school and college.

**Wendy Lawrence
Trustee RSI
ACTION;
Nottingham &
East Midlands RSI
Support Group
Coordinator**

Your excellent and informative book is much-needed. It helps to back up the guidance we produce, which aims to encourage best practice and highlights the danger of Work Related Upper Limb Disorders (WRULD).

**Sarah Moore,
Musculoskeletal Disorder Policy Unit
Health and Safety Executive (HSE UK)**

RSI
Repetitive Strain Injury

RSI is on the increase globally. This coincides with the boom of modern technology.

Did you know...
- In 2005 one out of fifty workers in the UK had RSI?
- Anyone using a computer or other modern technologies is a candidate for RSI
- **RSI can be avoided**

This book's main focus is on PREVENTION -
How to avoid RSI

Opportunities and dangers facing the young are addressed in the section, *Children Beware*.

There are anwers to *Frequently asked questions* on RSI, and practical guidance is given on what to do if you've got it.

The chance to explore more in-depth information is offered in the section *Digging deeper*

An extensive reference section provides a window onto the wider world.

Finally on the last page there is a useful *Summary on*

How to avoid RSI.

RSI
Repetitive Strain Injury

How to avoid it
And what to do if you've got it

Who will win – You or the Mouse?

Tonia Cope Bowley
Illustrated by William Harding

First published in Canada 2006 by Tonia Cope Bowley.
The moral right of Tonia Cope Bowley to be identified as the author of this work has been asserted.

Designed in Toronto, Canada by Adlibbed ltd.
Printed and bound by Lightningsource in the US or the UK.

ISBN:1-897312-23-7

Publish and be Damned helps writers publish their books. Ourservice uses a series of automated tools to design and print your book on-demand, eliminating the need for large print runs and inventory costs. Now, there's nothing stopping you getting your book into print quickly and easily.

For more information or to visit our book store please visit us at www.pabd.com

Why the Mouse?

The Mouse is everywhere!

The furry kind was on this planet long before we arrived. He was here to welcome and attract us, to taunt and outwit us, down through the centuries.

Recently the Mouse put on a non-furry guise as he entered the world of the microchip. It is now by far the most commonly used non-keyboard computer input device. 'All current software has become mouse driven and 30% of the average time spent using a keyboard involves the mouse' (1).

Today most people working with a mouse have no awareness of the hidden dangers. They have not had training on how to use it safely, nor on other aspects of modern technology. To make matters worse many people work for long hours without taking breaks usually because they are fascinated by their work, or are trying to meet deadlines. This too can contribute towards a debilitating Repetitive Strain Injury downfall.

The principles outlined in this book will help you to avoid the Mousetraps. I hope you will win!

Credits

This book was born out of the inspiration and help of a galaxy of people. Some merit special mention:

Stephen Bowley, for his support and for taking on the giant's share of the domestic tasks of our home and family when RSI was at its worst; my children Adam and David for doing extra duties and for keeping me amused.

Those with medical and holistic competences who lead and steady me up the slippery slope to recovery: Dr A Chivers, Dr N G Kostopoulos, Dr J Sorrel, Professor B P Wordsworth.

Several people who commented on various drafts, notably: Grace Townshend, medical editor and my editor-in-chief, who tirelessly trawled through draft after draft providing enhancing suggestions; Andy Chivers, GP; Elsa Christie, (former) Head Teacher, Unicorn School; Sarah Moore, HSE Directorate; Wendy Lawrence, RSI Action Trustee; Simon Griffiths, Osteopath; Elizabeth Walker, Senior Alexander Teacher; Barbara Cullinan and Alex Lamb, Physiotherapists; Dr Paul MacLoughlin, Consultant in Occupational Medicine, and RSI author; Adam Bowley, who at the age of 13 said with 'cool' gusto, when he'd read the draft: 'Go for it Mummy!'; Jenny Couzyn and Meshack Khosa great encouragers; and latterly Tim Roberts of Keytools, whose insights inspired just-in-time significant improvements; Chris Kelly, graduating D.Phil student, for checking the references with witty diligence!

MIT for their excellent RSI Information Pages, (2) which inspired the mouse-theme of this book.

Last but not least thanks are due to my illustrator, William Harding, for bringing life, humour and light to a somewhat sombre subject!

To the galaxy – thank you.

For Opti Munro

and You

Foreword

I am delighted to recommend this book. Tonia Cope Bowley is an expert patient whose personal experience combined with rigorous scientific enquiry has resulted in a book which will help sufferers and clinicians alike. It will give those at risk of RSI the chance to avoid it and empower those with symptoms to improve the situation.

RSI is one of those medical conditions for which there are no diagnostic tests, no cure and a very uncertain course. In addition, patients risk being labelled as having psychosomatic symptoms or dismissed as suffering from stress. We are still relatively ignorant about the causes of RSI but one crucial ingredient is the work environment.

RSI sufferers have often had to take assertive action themselves to achieve the necessary change in their work environment. Such a process is always stressful and can be confrontational. This book will help people through that process and give them strength to see it through. While the microchip can be seen as the prime cause of RSI, so also it can bring relief through speech recognition and better pointing devices for example. It is enormously gratifying that government grants can equip sufferers with ergonomic aids, but many fail to claim because of ignorance. Again this book will help people obtain appropriate equipment.

As employers wake up to the scale of the problem of RSI, this book takes us nearer a time when RSI will be designed out of our lives.

Dr Andy Chivers, GP,
Oxford City Primary Care Trust
Executive Committee Chair

Contents

vi

Note on the Case Studies

These tell the RSI stories of 'real' people known to the author, reported in the media, the press, magazines or told in contemporary books. In some instances the name has been changed to protect the privacy of that person.

In all cases the source can be verified.

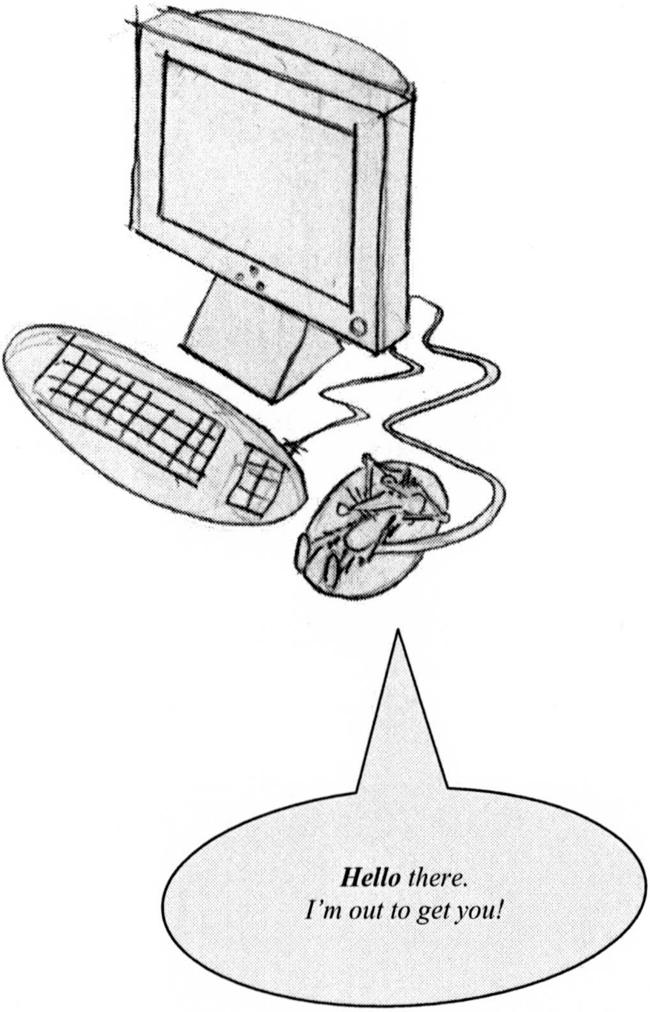
Hello *there.*
I'm out to get you!

A. Introduction

A message for you

In this age small is big! The microchip is mighty and globally affecting our lives – in the way we work, play and live. But do you know that amongst the exciting and growing opportunities, there lurk hidden but avoidable health hazards?

- *If you use computers, computer games, mobile phones etc., your health could be at risk. At worst you could suffer permanent and debilitating damage. The good news is that if you are aware of the dangers and work wisely, you should be OK.*
- *Whatever your work, if it includes repetitive actions as experienced by say hairdressers, electricians, or musicians, you too may be in danger of getting RSI.*
- *If you are experiencing pain while, or after using a mouse, computer keyboard, games console etc., seek professional help and make any advised adjustments quickly.*
- *If you are responsible for others at work, or in education, you are responsibile for their safety which includes providing a healthy working environment as spelt out by the UK Health and Safety Executive (3).*

*This book will help **you** to to understand how to avoid **Repetitive Strain Injury (RSI)** and what to do if you've got it. Also it points to many diffferent soures of help.*

Prevention is a million times better than cure – read on!

Tonia Cope Bowley
Oxford, 2006

1. Purpose

My aim is to introduce RSI, what it is, how to avoid getting it, and what to do if it strikes. You need to stay healthy in this microchip age to enjoy its benefits. The RSI danger is real!

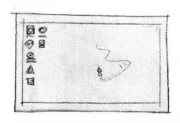

Did you know?

<u>In the UK - in 2002</u>
5.4 million work days were lost in sick leave due to RSI
<u>In 2003</u>
1 in 50 workers had an RSI. Cases are increasing.
6 people lost their jobs every day due to RSI　　　*(4)*
<u>By Nov. 2004</u> *RSI (with stress and back strains) was in the top 3 health hazards in the UK workplace (5, 6)*

It is my hope that these pages will stir you to think about how you use technology so that you do not put yourself at risk of damage.

Technology is replaceable – You are not!

2. My story

My career involved working daily with computers for nearly thirty years. A few years ago, through lack of awareness and pressures of work, I fell victim to RSI.

The mouse was my downfall coupled with a poor workstation set-up, long hours at a computer over extended periods, too few breaks and no 'warm-ups'. Then there were lengthy delays before recommended changes were made. Trouble was invited!

Until RSI struck I was unaware it existed.
So I did not recognise early symptoms, or know how to prevent the problem from becoming debilitating. Instead I worked on trying to ignore the increasing pain in my hands and arms.

Had I known what I know now I may not have met this setback. The consequences are long-term and serious. After four years of assorted remedial therapies under various specialists, searching out information, stopping and starting work, adapting my office, home and surroundings, my only option, in 2001, was to take medical retirement and leave the job I found fulfilling.

For some time I avoided using a keyboard or mouse. Improvement began slowly hand in hand with setbacks! I discovered I had to keep moving forward in the right direction keeping my eye on the goal of recovery. Gradually I got there – well almost!

5

Now I try to live a more balanced lifestyle and still avoid repetitive actions and carrying heavy items as much as possible.

I am not an ergonomic specialist nor am I medically qualified but I have consulted various experts who have read, and made contributions to these pages.

3. Ignorance to enlightenment

RSI is as old as the hills. It has eroded the lives of many whose work involved daily intensive repetitive hand movements. Today with the increasing technological revolution it has become a growing global menace. Many children and adults are in its disabling grip.

RSI costs organisations and countries billions a year (Chapter 43) Yet, RSI is preventable. To avoid it you must know the facts. You should heed the warning signs, take professional advice and carry out corrective action.

You must know yourself, your limitations and how best your body works, and take note and act when it speaks to you.

Until recently we have lived in a sea of RSI-ignorance but the tide is on the turn. Computers, software packages and websites come with health warnings like: 'Use of the keyboard or mouse may be linked to serious injuries or disorder'. Microsoft's website (7) has a Healthy Computing Guide. The former RSI Association's website (8), currently hosted by Keytools (9), has a range of information on causes, treatments, research findings, legal issues etc. The annual RSI Awareness Day (10) highlights research findings, and keeps a public focus on RSI. In fact there is a pending information avalanche!

Yet, there remains widespread ignorance of RSI in schools, higher education institutions, the workplace, and among individuals. But the number of people who work with computers and experience RSI in varying degrees is rising rapidly. This is hardly surprising when you realise that 'those working on computers may carry out as many as 25,000 fine hand movements an hour under employer pressure or in order to achieve a bonus level. Work-related upper limb disorders (WRULD / RSI) are likely to develop when keystrokes exceed 10,000 per hour' (11).
Amongst those with RSI I know personally are professors, students, architects, consultants, librarians, editors, researchers, web-designers and a nun! Non-computer victims include hairdressers and electricians.

I am constantly asked for information and help by those who have, or know someone with RSI. This motivated me to write the original version of this book (using Voice activated software (12)). I sent copies to top decision makers at Oxford University, and gave away books at my retirement reception. These have travelled far and wide. Feedback with comments like 'I read your book in the nick of time, took action and now I am fine', and continuing requests to publish, persuaded me to revise this book for wider circulation.

7

I cannot claim originality for much of the content. However I have tried to distill the most useful bits I have learnt from those who have RSI, medical advisors and through my own experience. I have drawn heavily on readily available information on the Internet, in books and other publications.

In this book:

- ❏ *We start off with 'Answers to Frequently asked questions on RSI', including what to do if you've got it*
- ❏ *The essential basics on prevention are in the section 'How to avoid RSI'*
- ❏ *A special focus on IT dangers for the young follows in 'Children beware!'*
- ❏ *The opportunity to explore more in-depth information is offered in 'Digging deeper'*
- ❏ *A window onto the wider world is provided in 'References and further reading'*
- ❏ *and finally on the last page there is a Summary on How to avoid RSI.*

Research into RSI is young but growing fast so it is well worth searching the Internet for the latest findings.

B. Frequently asked questions on RSI

9

4. What is RSI?

Repetitive Strain Injury (RSI) is an umbrella term for a number of overuse injuries affecting the soft tissue (muscles, tendons, and nerves) of the neck, the upper and lower back, chest, shoulders, arms, elbows and hands.

Unlike strains and sprains, which usually result from a single incident (acute trauma), repetitive strain injuries develop slowly as a result of repetitive movement in combination with other forms of structural or fascial strain (see chapter 42). If allowed to progress, RSI can develop into a permanent disability).

There are two types:

Specific named conditions such as tenosynovitis and carpal tunnel syndrome (there are more than 20 known disorders of the musculoskeletal system).

RSI is also known as:
NSPS - Non-Specific Pain Syndrome
MSD - Muscular Skeletal Disorder
OOS - Occupational Overuse Syndrome
CTD - Cumulative Trauma Disorder
ULD - Upper Limb Disorder
WRULD – Work-Related
Upper Limb Disorder
And other names by the score,
(see Chapter 37).

Confused?

Diffuse RSI where there is no clear-cut diagnosis but a range of symptoms exist (also known as Non Specific Pain Syndrome (NSPS).

5. Who is at risk?

No one is immune from developing RSI though some are more prone than others. Whether or not you will develop RSI depends on a combination of factors – how you work, how long you work, activities outside work and your general health. Australian researchers find women are more prone (13). Women doing two jobs are possibly more at risk if recovery time is not built into their day. Several experts report that the conscientious, and anyone doing highly repetitive work, are at risk.

The biggest risk group are those who use (overuse) modern technology in any shape or size.

Since the mid 1980s a mighty army of microchips started marching into offices and sitting on workers' desks, invading homes, and more recently overrunning schools and educational bodies. International reports claim computers are the main cause of RSI (14).

Young people are at great risk. The effect on their adult lives is as yet unknown, (see Section D). What is clear is that the problem is increasing on a global scale.

One hazard is the lure of the job. The more appealing a task, and the more you work to deadlines, the more likely you are to lose track of time. Also the less likely you are to become aware of developing fatigue and discomfort and the less likely you are to take well-timed breaks (15).

6. What causes RSI?

RSI is caused by a combination of factors including overuse and repetition, forceful movements on the keyboard, stress, working in cold conditions, awkward or static posture and insufficient recovery time.

'Use of a mouse or keyboard can lead to persistent muscle fatigue, tendon inflammation, compression of nerves, and subsequent disability that in some cases may be permanent' (16).

Then one morning I woke up to find ...

The onset of RSI may creep up in a sneaky fashion to catch you unawares. This could be the case even after using computers for years.

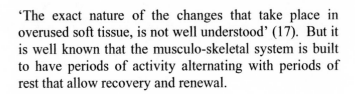

It could happen to you!

'The exact nature of the changes that take place in overused soft tissue, is not well understood' (17). But it is well known that the musculo-skeletal system is built to have periods of activity alternating with periods of rest that allow recovery and renewal.

'Working at the computer subjects certain part of the body to static postures while other parts move incessantly. Both static postures and constant activity can cause first microscopic and then macroscopic damage to biologic tissues' (16, and see Chapter 39).

13

Contributory factors include:

❏ **Repetition** – of small, rapid movements such as keying or mousing, for prolonged periods

❏ **Static and/or poor posture** – working, sometimes compulsively, in the same position, or awkward posture for long stretches of time

❏ **Poor workstation setup** – a table / chair ratio that is wrong for you and cannot be adjusted for you to work comfortably, bad lighting, etc

❏ **Badly designed hardware** – mouse, keyboard etc. The mouse is usually placed to the side of the keyboard so you have to reach out to use it. This puts twice as much stress on the neck, arm and shoulders as it would if were in the centre

❏ **Force** – using excessive force particularly on the keyboard or by gripping the mouse

❏ **Too few breaks** and changes of activity to allow your body to recover from an activity

❏ **Working in cold conditions** adds to the risk

❏ **Pushing yourself** too hard with insufficient rest

❏ **Stress** in any form can accelerate the problem

❏ **Unsympathetic management** may discourage early reporting of RSI symptoms leaving you unsure of which way to turn.

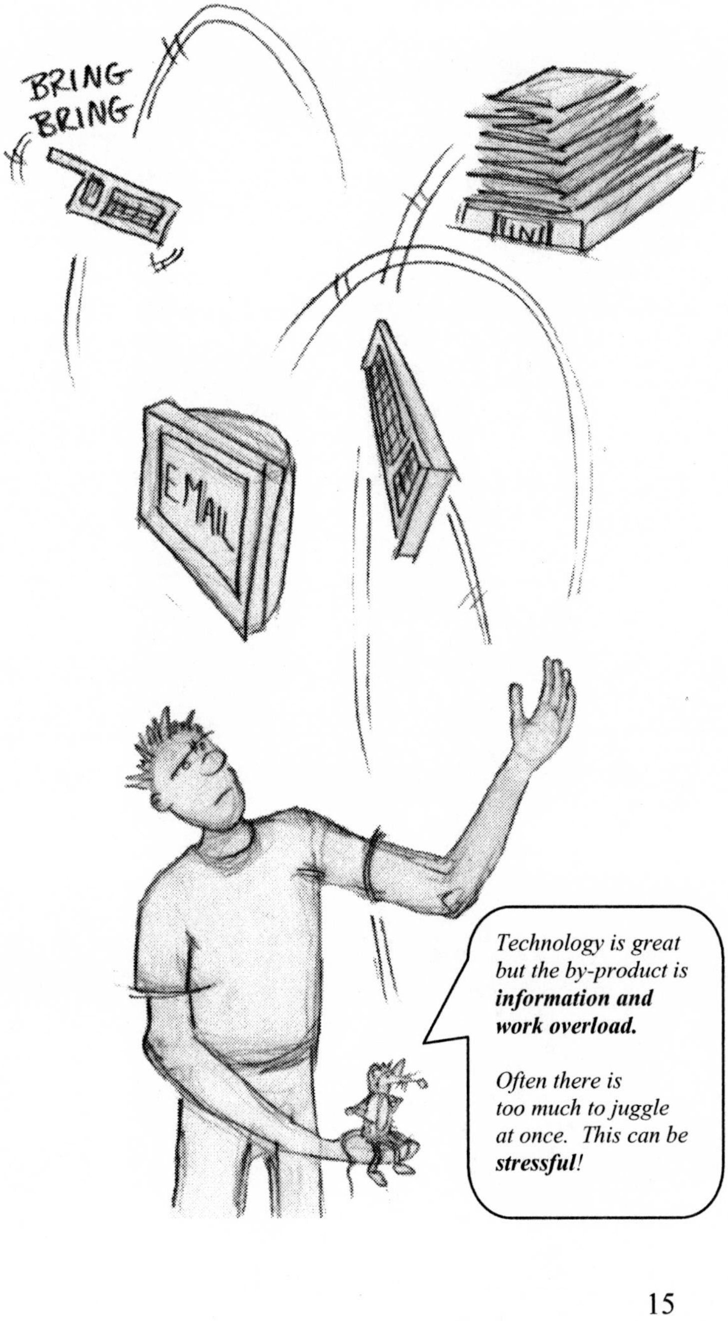
BRING
BRING
EMAIL
Technology is great but the by-product is **information and work overload.**
Often there is too much to juggle at once. This can be **stressful**!

7. Where does it hurt?

Symptoms and warning signs

The symptoms of RSI include pain, muscle aches or spasm, tenderness, swelling, crepitus (creaking during movement), tingling, and numbness. It may occur anywhere in the upper limbs, neck or back. Pain is often worse at night or when resting. Advanced symptoms in your hands include loss of strength, clumsiness and decreased coordination. Even simple tasks like buttoning a shirt, turning a door handle, brushing your teeth, or carrying things may prove difficult.

Symptoms may appear in any order and at any stage in the development of an injury and may not appear immediately after the activity causing the problem. Pain may be referred – i.e. it may not be felt where the actual stress is occurring.

If you wake up at night with painful or 'burning' hands or arms, pain in the elbow or shoulder, it could be a sign of RSI as a result of keying or mousing.

Loss of sleep induced by pain will add to your fatigue and vulnerability.

In general, the more intense the symptoms, the more often you experience these and the longer they last, the more serious your injury is likely to be. A severe injury can develop only weeks after symptoms appear, or it may take years (3, 8).

16

If you are experiencing any of these symptoms do not ignore them.

ACT!

Contact your GP or a medical expert immediately. Early diagnosis, professional help and treatment may solve your problem once and for all. Delay could result in more permanent damage.

8. What can you do if you hurt?

When your body starts hurting
STOP
what you are doing.

> **Listen**
> *when your body tries to tell you something is wrong.*
> ***Pain is a warning signal.***
> *Your body whispers to you.*
> *If you ignore the whispers, it talks.*
> *If you ignore the talking, it shouts.*
> *Eventually it will go on strike and refuse to work at all.*
> Bunny Martin (18)

DO

❑ **See a doctor** as soon as possible

❑ Don't wait for the condition to become aggravated. **Early treatment is vital** for overuse injuries

❑ **'Once RSI reaches an advanced state** full recovery may be a very long process of months or even years' (7)

❑ **If the doctor doesn't know much about RSI** ask to be referred to someone who does

18

❑ **Keep a log** using headings like:

Date: What I did: What I noticed.

This will be helpful to you and your medical advisors in understanding your particular problem and in arriving at a diagnosis

❑ **Tell your employer** or the person in charge (back this up in writing) and ask to see an Occupational Health Advisor (or equivalent) for an assessment

❑ **Ask for a professional ergonomic advisor** to see your worksite if you are not satisfied with the assessment (not all Health and Safety people are adequately qualified). In some countries support is available if your condition affects the kind of work you do. For example, in the UK, if your problem affects your work, and is likely to last 12 months or more, you can get help from Access to Work – from Job Centre Plus at the Dept. of Work and Pensions (19)

❑ **Be willing to change.** To recover it is virtually certain you will need to change at least some of your work patterns. Take advice and implement recommended changes straight away. Don't continue bad habits that are harmful to you. You may need to change some of your equipment

❑ **Check out guidelines for good workstation/** work setup (Chapters 16–22)

❑ **Pay attention to your posture** and keep your body movements free (Chapter 17)

❑ **Find out about adaptive equipment** –
for example alternative input devices like touch
pads, keyboards, mice, tracker balls and voice
recognition software (see Chapters 19, 20, 26).
Using a pen or pencil with a bigger diameter can
make all the difference to your writing with
greater comfort

❑ **Relax** – find ways that help you

❑ **Take regular exercises** to keep your body and
mind strong and flexible – like walking (gently),
jogging, swimming, water aerobics or anything
else you find helpful

❑ **Share your experience** and learn from others
It could benefit you to join a support group

❑ **Explore** different medical treatments including exercises and stretches. Some examples:

- o A physiotherapist may give you various on the spot treatments and teach you exercises to strengthen particular muscles

- o You can create your own exercise routines demonstrated in many of the self help books – for example, reference 11

- o If you are online you can explore one of the ergonomic software packages. Many offer a free demonstration version so you can try before you buy. This is explored in more detail in Chapter 12

- o Be open to alternative therapies (Chapters 9 and 42)

❑ **Learn more about RSI** – there are many helpful books, an explosion of RSI-related sites on the Internet and electronic mailing lists

❑ **Persevere**, be patient and have a positive attitude.

Worth noting

- ❑ Most people who experience RSI make a satisfactory recovery
- ❑ The earlier the problem is addressed the greater the chance of full recovery
- ❑ Only 3%–4% suffer long-term problems (14).

DON'T

- ❏ **Take painkillers** just to mask your symptoms and continue working

- ❏ **Panic** if you feel you are starting RSI – do something about it

- ❏ **Don't be pushed** into making hasty decisions about giving up work or going back too soon

- ❏ **Rush back to work** too soon after time off and undo your progress.

You may find that the job you found second nature has become exhausting and overwhelming. You probably need to modify what you do and how you do it.

If you simply fall back into the habits that caused your problem you could end up in a worse state.

Perhaps the time has come for you to consider changing your job.

23

Case Study 1   Need for a diagnosis

In July 2005 an email arrived in my inbox from my friend Anne. For five years she'd worked in one of the world's largest countries for an international aid organisation. Currently in a disaster area, she developed health policy; project managed, and advised Government. Her 12-hour days included 8 hours on a laptop in poor conditions, and also texting.

Extract from Anne's email on 24 July 2005
*I have 10 weeks to go. My left shoulder is very sore, I have severe pain around my right shoulder, fingers on that hand tingle and are a bit numb, and a dull pain is up that arm. I lack apt medical help but I have sorted out postural issues as far as I can and had massage. I do not have your book here (*note: Anne had a draft of this book*) so please offer advice.*

Extract from my reply.
The term RSI covers over 20 ailments. You may have more than one. Recently someone with similar symptoms asked me for help. Her self diagnosis was RSI, but tests showed unrelated surgery had upset the muscle balance in her left shoulder. Physio helped restore full use. Clearly, lay opinions aren't enough. <u>You must get a diagnosis.</u> For now <u>STOP!</u> <u>Take breaks</u> often. You are more important than your work!

Contributory factors and outcome
For 5 years Anne thrived on her work but in March she'd picked up a bug and her reserve was low. Driven by deadlines, pressures from benefactors, colleagues, and her own commitment, she kept working when she knew she should stop. After her email she took 2 weeks holiday.

Anne met her targets at great cost to herself. Now that she is back in the UK, pain is constant, and tasks like dressing, holding a phone, etc, are hard. She cannot drive or garden. At night the pain wakes her. She is seeking medical help and I hope she'll recover. Had she stopped earlier these severe complications may have been avoided.

9. How can you recover?

This chapter assumes you have signs of developing RSI or have a persistent problem. If you have not done so consult a medical expert to get a diagnosis.

Arriving at a diagnosis might not be straightforward if you do not have any recognizable clinical features. You may need to be referred to a specialist with experience in RSI who will also consider your medical history and total lifestyle. There are some conditions that can complicate upper limb disorders. You may need treatment and help to find the best way forward for you.

> *The most important help is the help you give yourself. Don't wait for someone else to sort out your RSI. Be proactive. Take control of your life and your recovery programme.*
> *Let RSI come to mean:*
> - *Reassess your circumstances*
> - *Seek out appropriate help*
> - *Implement changes quickly*

An RSI condition (and there are 20 or more RSI disorders of the musculo-skeletal system) may have built up over a long period of overuse – months or years – before pain is felt.

It is possible that muscles, tendons and nerves have become inflamed and/or damaged, and as a result blood flow has been restricted in some areas making the problem worse (Chapters 39).

Everyone is different. Individual circumstances and the causes of RSI are different. What works for one person may not work for someone else. There is no one answer to recovering from RSI, but there is a lot that can help.

a.   Working and lifestyle changes

If you suspect you have, or are developing RSI, see a doctor straight away and avoid any activities that aggravate your pain. If your hands are painful due to excessive use of a computer, then household tasks like peeling and chopping vegetables, cleaning, ironing, washing dishes, carrying heavy shopping, gardening, driving, etc (Chapter 9g, 9h) may worsen your condition and should be minimised or avoided. Arduous though this may seem, it is worth it if it means you will recover.

Review your life – your work/play balance, equipment you use, and how long you spend each day or week using this. Think about the ergonomics of how you go about your work (Section C, Chapter 38). *Ergonomics is about designing or adapting equipment and the job to suit you and not the other way round.*

You may need to change your living patterns and possibly your job. 'Many after developing RSI retrain in an area of work that will not worsen their RSI. This can be stressful but may provide a new challenge' (20). Two examples of real people who experienced severe RSI but who are now both in successful careers – one in a new career, the other in the same one – are given in Case Studies 2 and 4.

Case Study 2   Career change beats RSI

RSI strikes Cambridge University student

Five years ago 25-year-old Pia wondered if she'd ever work again. Pain started in her second year at Cambridge University while she was sitting on an ordinary chair using a PC. Soon she was unable to write and had to dictate her finals. She took time off to recover.

Within the first year in her first job widespread pain and fatigue overwhelmed Pia. Nothing helped until she went for career counselling, and to a pain clinic. The counselling identified the jobs she was suited to, and that required limited time on the keyboard. Through the pain clinic she learnt that the pain in her wrists came from her neck and upper back and that better posture, regular exercise and stretching would keep the pain at bay.

Pia took a job in marketing with a firm that takes health and safety seriously and invests in workers' well being. Her firm provided her with suitable furniture and anything they understood would help her. Their support made all the difference to Pia's progress. Pia regained her zest for life thanks due largely to a self-disciplined regime of exercise and time management.

(For full article see (21))

2 years on
Pia's husband, who also suffers from RSI, wrote: "Both of us manage our various RSI-style problems – via regular chiropractic appointments, sports massage, stretches and exercise - and as a result are both working full time and very hard. I now use my chiropractor as a mechanic to keep my body going, when we have a lot of work on, as we do at the moment."

(Email 22 April 2005)

27

b. Treatment and rehabilitation

The aim of treatment is to restore normal health. Achieving this depends on early reporting of the ailment, the severity of the condition and gaining a diagnosis. The outcome of treatments (and there may be more than one) leads to total recovery in the best case. In the worst case, where RSI has been neglected for too long, or the person fails to change poor working conditions, permanent disability could result.

Treatments vary. Finding the right one or a combination may be a case of trial and error. Start by seeking to eliminate the root causes.

What you can do immediately is rest the affected areas. This does not mean doing nothing with your hands, which could result in muscle wastage over time. Rather, avoid activities causing the problem or irritating it like using the keyboard, mouse, or texting.

You should continue doing other things as normally as possible.

You may be recommended appropriate exercises or gentle stretching to improve your posture and circulation, relieve pain and restore strength (see Chapter 12).

It may suit you to take Alexander Technique lessons which teach good use of your total self, and enable you to unlearn unhealthy and harmful habits, which may have developed over years. Alternatively Pilates, Yoga, etc, may be appropriate (see Chapter 42).

Once you know the principles of what to do, you can probably manage your own treatment program.

c. Listen to your pain

Pain is a warning signal.
It is a messenger bringing news
that something is wrong.

This is crazy!
I wish. I wish. I wish …
I'd listened to the whispers of
the messenger. Now I'm
deafened by his shouts!

A typical modern
response
to pain is to deaden
and obscure it by
taking a pill,
but this approach
deals with the
symptoms and not
with the problem.

We dare not turn off
the warning system
without first listening
to the warning.

Pain is something only you feel and this makes it difficult to tell others just how bad it is. This is especially true with RSI as you may continue to look healthy while in considerable pain.

'The most common type of pain is acute pain, which is usually temporary. If you continue to work with acute pain, tendons, muscles or joints may become inflamed. If you rest and obtain appropriate treatment your acute pain usually goes away' (22). If you don't attend to your pain it will in time become more complex, chronic pain.

d. Managing pain

Pain may warn of something beginning to go wrong. Alternatively pain may indicate a problem that has developed over years or months, so treating the pain, and the cause, may not result in an overnight solution.

But how can you deal with your pain be it mild or unbearable? First seek professional advice on the best methods for you. There is a lot of immediate help on the Internet and in books, see for example, The British Pain Society website (23). The US MIT website (2) also has useful information. Sharon Butler (24) offers well-illustrated gentle stretches designed to relieve pain in any specific part of the upper body. Many people have found this method helpful.

Take responsibility for yourself
The idea is to take responsibility for yourself – learn how to manage your pain. You may need help in getting to this point. Evidence shows that people who take an active role in understanding and managing their own pain do better than those who rely solely on others.

Take time to understand the nature of pain and what affects it like the type and level of activity, stress and negative thinking. And take one step at a time. Almost certainly your pain, although it may appear to have arrived overnight, may have been developing for years. It is therefore unlikely that it will resolve overnight.

Try to minimise stress – pain and stress feed off each other. Learn to relax your mind and body, pace yourself, and set reasonable goals as part of your everyday life.

What you should not do is take painkillers while carrying on working when you have pain, in your hands, arms, neck etc. This is courting disaster – disaster that is avoidable, especially when catching the problem early can eliminate most causes. The doctor managing your recovery may suggest the use of pain relief or muscle relaxants for limited periods under supervision.

Not everyone with RSI has pain. Some experience varying forms of numbness or incapacity. There is a range of pain – achy, sharp, localised, generalised, constant or intermittent, burning or throbbing.

The good news is
'90% of all the pains people suffer are short-term pains: correctable situations that call for medication, rest, or a change in a person's lifestyle' (27).

Chronic pain
For those with chronic pain there are clinics that offer a holistic approach to pain management, such as St Thomas' Hospital, London (25), and Suparna Damany's clinic, Pennsylvania, United States (26).

Learn to look after yourself
You are a unique and valuable person no matter what you are going through. Don't isolate yourself and remember to give yourself some treats! Stay positive – you *can* get better.

e. Pacing

This is a recovery method often recommended by pain clinics. The main points are that you should:

1. Plan ahead
2. Keep a pain management diary
3. Take short and frequent breaks
4. Gradually increase the amount you do
5. Break up tasks into smaller pieces

It requires you discover your body's baseline tolerances for activities that lead to pain and then work out how much you can manage on good days and on bad days in your normal lifestyle.

Look at what you have to do – essential activities (walking, sitting etc.); domestic activities (household stuff etc.); and work activities (writing, computer work, etc.). Prioritise your activities and gradually move forward, adjusting your baseline according to your progress.

There is more to pacing than space allows here. There is a fuller explanation in some books, for example: *Coping successfully with RSI* (28).

On the road to recovery you are bound to have ups and downs. Don't be discouraged by setbacks but try to find out the cause and adjust your activities. Try to look on these setbacks as part of your recovery learning curve. In hill country for every down there is an up!

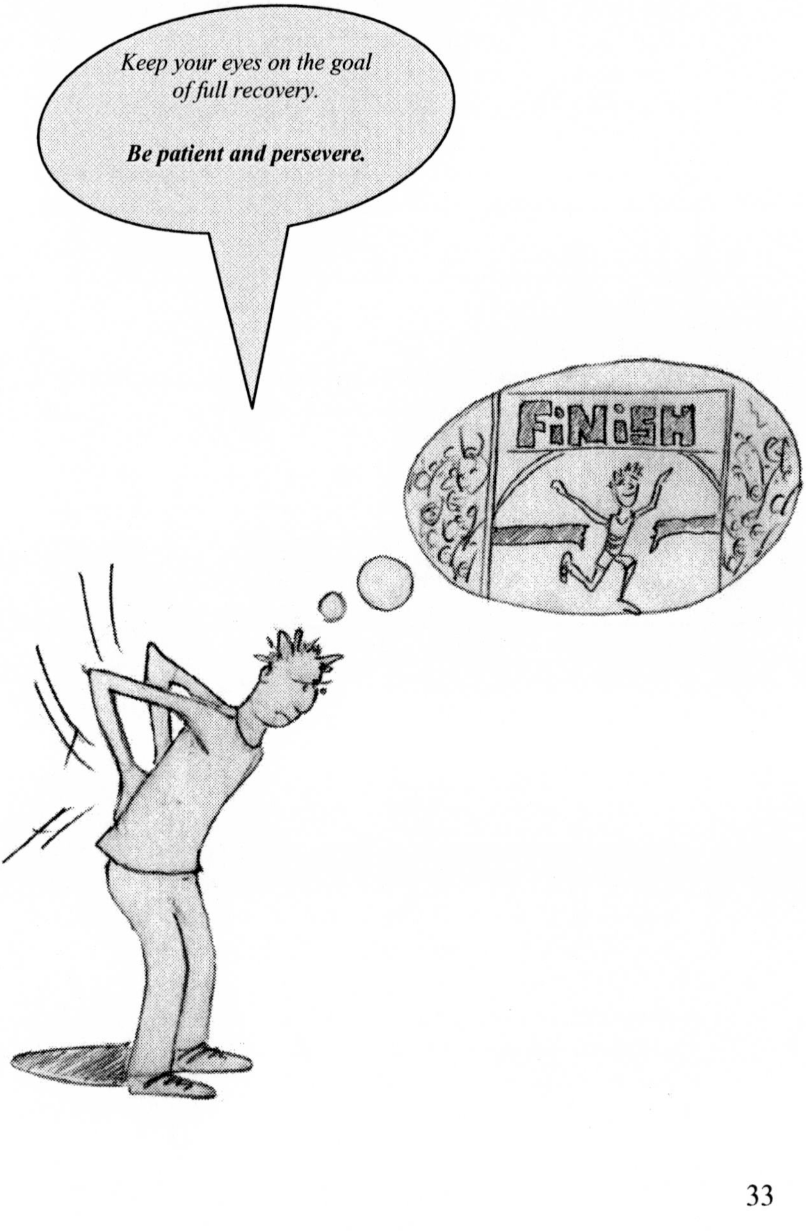
Keep your eyes on the goal of full recovery.
Be patient and persevere.
FiNiSH

f. Ways to help yourself

There are many ways to help yourself. Rather than focusing on the painful areas alone try a more holistic approach. Exercise, relaxation, pacing yourself, and changing the way you do some things, are key ingredients. In short, move towards a more balanced lifestyle. It may take time to achieve. Below are some of the components.

❑ **Get sufficient rest**

❑ **Vary what you do.** Do work involving repetitive movements in short bursts alternating with something different

❑ **Improve your nutrition** and drink plenty of water. You need to keep your energy levels up

❑ **Take a leisurely warm bath** or shower

❑ **Apply hot or cold packs** – there are various methods

One, suggested by Dr N G Kostopoulos (former Harley Street Specialist now at the Holistic Health Centre in Athens) (29), is to soak your hands and lower arms alternately in very hot/very cold water (30 seconds each) for a 5-minute cycle. To end with, soak in highly saline very hot water (1/2 cup of salt in sink full of water) for a further 5 minutes. This can be done to ease discomfort just before going to bed, if woken by pain in the night, or during the day. *(This method may not suit everyone – it does me – check with your medical advisor before trying this method.)*

❑   **Have gentle exercise** including stretching, walking, movement to music, jogging, swimming, water aerobics etc

❑   **Have a sauna and/or steam bath** before or after swimming

❑   **Tubigrip** can be worn over the wrist area for support and warmth. For added support wear more than one. (Tubigrip is available at most chemists. You can dye it a colour you like!)

❑   **Wrist splint (s) may be worn.** Use mainly at night to immobilise your wrist area. This is helpful for a limited period but check with your medical advisor. If worn permanently muscle wastage may result.
Off the shelf splints are available. Some RSI sufferers find that when pain is bad sleeping in a wrist splint brings considerable relief. Besides immobilising the wrist these splints keep the area warm, and the carpal tunnel, through which the blood vessels and nerves pass to the hands, open at a neutral position.

❑   **Take a course in The Alexander Technique**, the Bowen Technique, Pilates, Yoga, Tai Chi etc. or teach yourself the Hellerwork stretching method (24) and Chapter 42

❑   **Develop a positive attitude** to your RSI. A can-do approach will speed recovery

❑   **Take time to learn** more about how your body works. Dr Paul MacLoughlin has a well-illustrated chapter on Clinical Anatomy that is truly helpful (30). To develop a habit of healthy computer practice you need to be skilled at observing how you use your body – your head-neck-spine relationship, your joints and muscles etc. – and hence adapt to a healthier style of moving and sitting with effortlessness. It is not easy to do this on your own. One of the methods referred to in Chapter 42 may help

❑ **Install stretch-break monitoring software** on your computer. (Chapter 12). For example RSIGuard offers various options. Micropauses coax you to pause for a few seconds and prompt you think about *how* you are working. Longer breaks come with (demonstrated) exercises, at a time interval you have set. With the auto-click facility you point and the computer 'clicks', saving your hands. Stretch-break monitoring software provides immediate benefit. A trial version is free from the Keytools website (9).

g. Smart tips on adjusting your lifestyle

You can make many simple adjustments to improve your day to day living. The suggestions below are based on my own experience and those I know who have RSI.

First – as far as you can, avoid anything that adds stress to your sore hands, arms, etc.

At home (where possible)

❑ invest in a cleaner

❑ get someone to do your ironing – and buy non iron garments

❑ ignore the dust!

In the kitchen

If you live with others form a team! Delegate someone to do the shopping – or at least carry it. If you must shop use a shopping trolley. Supermarket staff will usually pack and load your shopping into your car.

Organise your 'team' to do the manual food preparation – lifting heavy pots and pans, peeling vegetables etc.
You can do the creative planning and cooking bit if that is what you enjoy! Don't be shy to ask. Most people love to help (usually even grumbling teenage kids behind their protest-masks!).

❑   **Washing up** – use a dishwasher

❑   **The kettle** – invest in a lightweight and easy to use model. Boil only the water you need

❑   **Saucepans** – invest in light ones

❑   **Food preparation** – use mechanical aids wherever possible – food processors, blenders, electric carving knives, cheese drum graters and the like

❑   **Vegetables** – potatoes – boil in the skins and if your hands are a big problem, don't even wash them! They clean themselves in the boiling

37

process and are then really easy to peel once cooked – or if clean leave the skins on if you prefer. Carrots and other root vegetables – wash then boil, steam, or roast whole. Greens, cauliflower etc – boil or steam whole then cut up when cooked. Cooked vegetables are much easier to cut up than raw ones and keep their flavour and goodness better

❑ **Meat, poultry, fish** – avoid buying whole if you have to cut them up yourself. Buy ready to eat pieces if you can

❑ **Aim for a balanced and nutritious diet.**

The Australian RSI association publication "Living with RSI/OOS" has a section in the appendix on RSI Friendly Recipes (31).

General activities

Using a telephone

If holding a traditional cord phone is difficult, try:

❑ Switching hands often

❑ Using a cordless phone – it allows more flexibility

❑ Using a headset

❑ Using a speaker phone

❑ Automatic or voice activated dialling.

Reading

❑ Read in a good light in a good posture so that you are not straining any muscles in the process

❑ Your chair should give you suitable support.

❑ Try sitting at a table with your book supported. Special reading chairs are available. For example 'Bookchair', styled as a small wooden deck chair, is designed to prop up a book or magazine on the table (32)

❑ Reading while seated – prop the book up using cushions, a lap tray, book stand, etc rather than hold it

❑ You may prefer to listen to Talking Books.

Driving

In the worst case, if your RSI is bad and your manual car has a difficult gear change etc, you may need to give up driving while your hands recover, or acquire an automatic model.

(I didn't / couldn't drive for over 2 years. Eventually when we needed to buy a new car we bought a second hand automatic with power steering. It was liberating and a great practical help as our children were small and needed transport to school.)

Where possible drive cars with these features:

❑ Automatic

❑ Power steering

❑   Central locking

❑   Power windows.

Opening doors

Heavy doors and those with stiff handles can present a real challenge to someone with RSI. It may prove impossible to open a door in the conventional manner. Try these tricks:

❑   Push the door using your feet, hips or shoulder

❑   Pull the door by standing close to it, grasp and turn the handle then and step back keeping your arm straight using it as a lever

❑   Wait at the door until someone comes and follow them through!

❑   If your door has a knob handle change it to a lever handle. This enables you to open the door with your elbow!

Shaking hands

This time honoured western tradition often proves painful to the RSI sufferer especially if the shaker has a grip like a vice.

Advice:

❑   DON'T shake hands!

❑   Find your own way of joking yourself out of the situation – hands behind your back and a big smile could do it.

Clapping

It is frustrating but true that clapping can be very painful for someone with RSI. So, don't! It is easy to just pretend to clap!

Carrying

- ❑ Use a rucksack rather than a shoulder bag – better balance

- ❑ Replace a handbag by a bum bag / money belt

- ❑ Avoid carrying more than is absolutely necessary

- ❑ Use both hands to carry and keep the 'load' close to your body

- ❑ Use a trolley when shopping.

Travelling

- ❑ Travel light – NO non essentials!

- ❑ Take only the luggage you can manage yourself

- ❑ Use bags or cases with wheels

- ❑ A small rucksack may be appropriate – some have wheels

- ❑ Tell your travel agent in advance if you will need help

- ❑ Allow extra time to avoid stressful situations.

Gardening

Gardening can give you a real boost. There is something special about working with the soil and seeing things push through and grow. Even a tiny patch or pot outside your front door can be satisfying. Flowers or small vegetables like lettuce can reward you and bring you satisfaction. You do need to take care however not to overdo it and aggravate your RSI.

❑ Enjoy what you do in the garden

❑ Work at your own pace

❑ Frequently change what you are doing

❑ Take breaks

❑ Use lightweight tools

❑ For pruning use ratchet secateurs

❑ Relax!

❑ You may well discover other adjustments of your own.

For a more detailed account on making adjustments to improve your day to day living see the Australian RSI association publication 'Living with RSI/OOS' (31).

h. Options for dealing with pain

❑ Acupuncture, acupressure

❑ Anti inflammatory tablets or a course of such

❑ Arnica cream rubbed on painful areas

❑ Ayurveda (Science-of life)
   (*Ancient holistic approach used widely in the East)*

❑ Chiropractic, osteopathy, hydrotherapy

❑ Complementary therapies (see Chapter 42)

❑ Massage including deep tissue massage

❑ Occupational therapy

❑ Pain clinics

❑ Physiotherapy

❑ Rheumatology

❑ Steroid injections

❑ Surgery (in limited cases)

❑ Trigger point therapy (33)

❑ Various homeopathic remedies

And more!

Remember there are no quick fixes. Your progress may not be as rapid as you'd like, but keep on keeping on. The tortoise will win in the end.

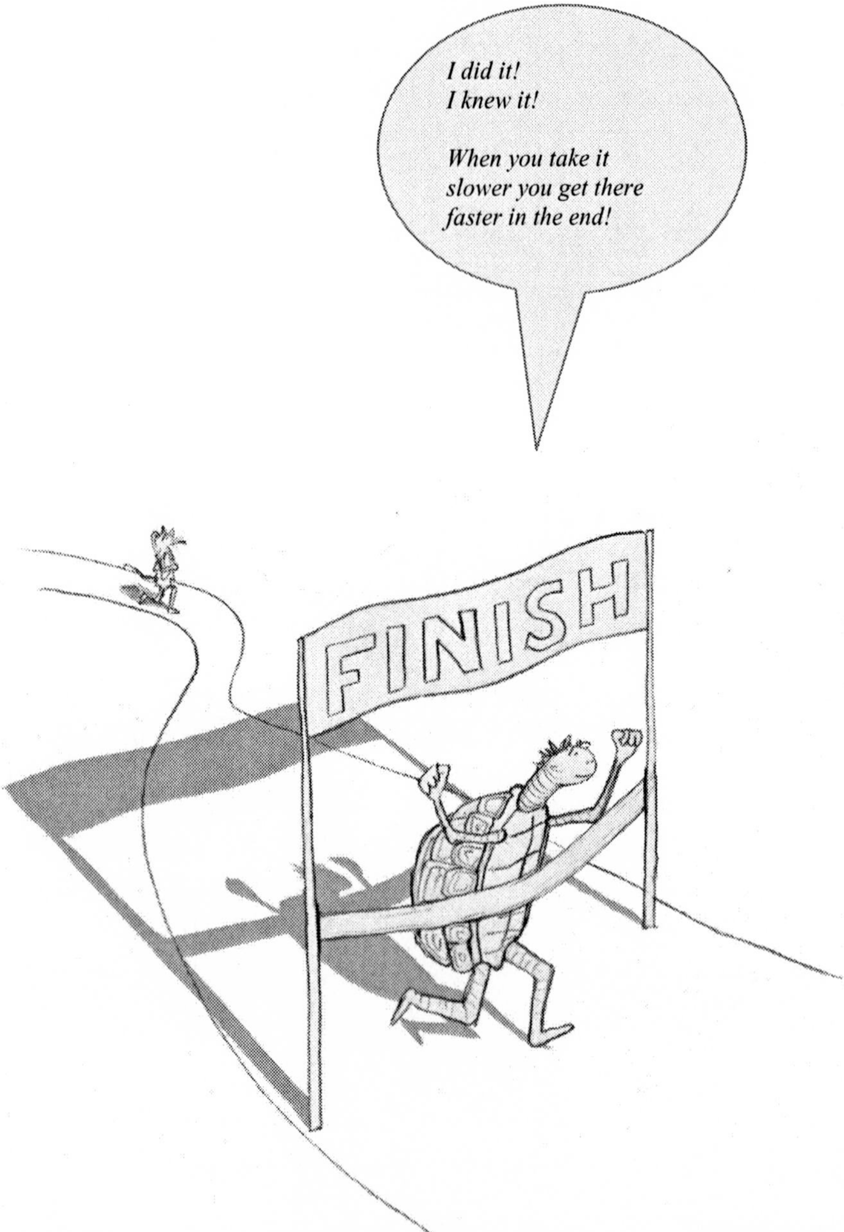
I did it!
I knew it!
When you take it slower you get there faster in the end!
FINISH

C. How to avoid RSI – Prevention

10. Develop good habit patterns

If you *really, really* want to achieve your goal I believe, more often than not, you can. But it may take longer than you planned. If however, you do not understand yourself, and the technological opportunities and constraints of the modern world, you could fail to achieve this goal. Something like RSI could stop you.

It won't ever happen to me! I thought.

*But I was wrong. I was so busy running, chasing my goals and deadlines, that I failed to see the trap and **lost** my tail.*

The old adage 'prevention is better than cure' applies. And, it is relatively easy to protect yourself from RSI.

Developing good habit patterns and an understanding of the balance between you, your lifestyle, and technology should put you on the winning side against the mouse.

But why is prevention of RSI given such a low priority? One reason is ignorance. Many people / organisations remain unaware that RSI exists and is on the increase. If they have heard of RSI they fail to understand, like the proverbial ostrich, that it could affect them. The costs in both monetary and physical terms can be high (See Chapter 43).

47

The problem is widespread. This trend began at the start of the eighties with the arrival of personal computers. New opportunities were suddenly available and everyone dived onto these microchip-wonders without thought of possible complications.

In little over 20 years computers, games consoles, mobile phones, the Internet, etc became commonplace. People rush to use these for long hours tapping, mousing or texting and kids pile onto games consoles. Most are ignorant of possibly developing disabling disorders unless they sit and type correctly, take breaks, and keep fit generally.

Awareness of the potential dangers of overuse, and the detrimental effects of poor habits, should be everyday knowledge. Isolated education programmes on RSI should rapidly evolve into national and local schemes. All technology users should be trained in its healthy use.

They need to be taught how to stop and think not only about their subject matter and the technology they are using, but also the whys and wherefores of leading a balanced lifestyle.

The least and the best we can do for the rising generations is to give them the opportunity to develop habit patterns that will help to keep them computer-fit for life!

Most important is to be able to recognise warning signs and to **STOP on amber**.

11. Pace yourself

Plan your work and play so that one activity isn't performed for extended periods. Limit the time spent working on the computer; vary working positions. Use different input devices to accomplish a task – eg keyboard, mouse, different kinds of mice, voice.

When tackling a long task at the computer change your position frequently and take short, regular breaks. Short frequent rests provide better protection than long breaks after working in a static position for hours. Get up and move around if you begin to feel any symptoms. Pause every so often and do some exercise. Installing a break monitoring programme will help.

When you take the time to attend to yourself you will find you get the job done faster! It is most important to plan your work so that you alternate sitting at your computer with mobile activities.

12. Exercises and stretches

Keep fit and supple. Recommended exercise for general health is a minimum of 20 minutes, five days a week.

Besides training, athletes, swimmers, and musicians all warm up regularly. Very few who use technology have even thought of warming up.

When exercising do the things you enjoy doing. It could be gardening, walking, swimming, dancing, vigorous housework, the gym or some combination.

Basic principles of exercising and stretching

- ***Counter balance***
  Start by stretching to balance the repetitive movements you have been doing. For example if your hands and fingers have been curled in towards the palm of your hand through repeated typing or mousing do a stretch or two to open up your hands and stretch your fingers

- ***Fun***
  There is nothing like fun to get you motivated. So find ways to have fun when exercising or stretching. Examples:
  * If it motivates you attach a pedometer to tell you how far you walk a day!
  * Play your favourite lively music while you work and dance or stretch to this as the mood takes you.

A lot is written about stretches, illustrated in books like Sharon Butler's *Conquering Carpal Tunnel Syndrome* (24). This is well illustrated with recommended sequences of stretches for any part of the body.

Software on avoiding RSI can be found on the Internet with many programs allowing you to watch-and-do!

Watch and DO
The newer sites show live, or animated examples allowing you to repeat what you see.

Examples:

The MIT *Website* (2) points to a series of well-illustrated hand exercises you can do at your desk before plunging into work. These can be downloaded, stuck up on the wall, and done anytime.

The e-stretch website (34) will get you started in a friendly way. Each exercise is explained and demonstrated so you can see what to do and choose to hear the instructions! The vital importance of hand-health is emphasised.

> ***Warm-up hand stretching***
> ***is a habit worth cultivating***

51

RSIGuard is (35) a modern sophisticated software suite that includes stretches during timely breaks, micro pauses, active click etc. You can choose which options you want to include as you set up the programme to suit you. It is an integrated approach to preventing and managing repetitive strain injury. You can download a trial version.

This is one of the most effective programs I have used and is what I currently use daily. Here is an example of what others think about RSIGuard taken from the Keytools website where you will find other examples.

Lofty praise for RSIGuard
★ ★ ★ ★ ★

RSIGuard is simply a magnificent program.

It's valuable not only to those with RSI, but to anyone who tends to hyper-focus: writers, programmers, scientists.

At times, I've found myself at work typing for nearly six hours not even knowing that the time has passed, forgetting to even eat. Then I get out of my chair and wonder why my shoulders and back are killing me!

With RSIGuard, just to be forced to look at the time was extremely valuable to me. It also lets me know when I'm losing it a little i.e., when I get angry because 15 seconds seems like too long a time to wait, I know that I need to step back.

I highly recommend RSIGuard to everyone who works hard. It'll keep your body and hands healthy!

Phillip S. Pang, M.D. Ph.D.

What is needed now is a cultural shift from ignorance and complacency to a **trendy stretch-culture!**

Try managing without using your hands even for one day and you will appreciate the value and importance of healthy hands.

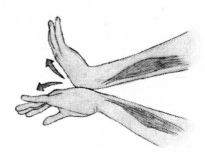

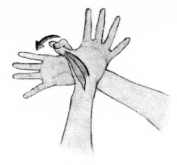

Hands are our unique and wonderful human instruments used in almost all we do.

Look after yours!

53

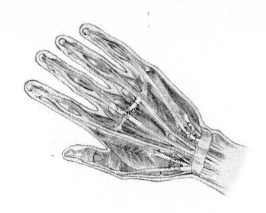

Did you know?

Fingers have no muscles themselves. This allows them to be slim and nimble. Tendons transfer force from muscles in the forearm and palm.

Scores of muscles in the upper arm, shoulder, neck and chest, and virtually throughout our entire upper torso reinforce hand activities. In fact seventy separate muscles contribute to hand movement (36).

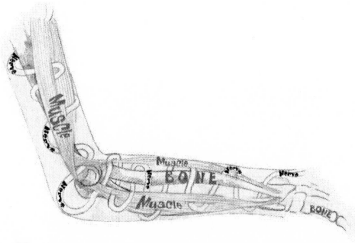

13. Take breaks

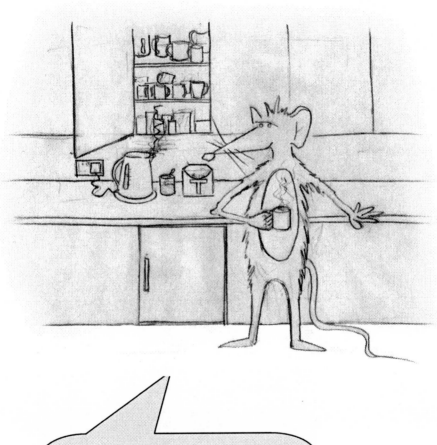

Bunny Martin, RSI Consultant, says
'If you wiggle a piece of electrical wire,
over and over again, for seven hours a day,
five days a week, it starts to fray and break.
The difference between the computer
and a human being is that
we're not robots and I can't unscrew your
arm and re-wire your wiring' (18).

Our bodies are not designed to remain static for long periods of time. But this happens all too easily when engrossed in a particular task on a computer.

As you become skilful in observing how you use your body it becomes easier to develop healthy computer practice. You will be able to adapt to a healthier style of moving and sitting. It is not easy to do this on your own. This is where break monitoring packages are invaluable in that they prompt you to pause and take a break. When circumstances dictate you can override this.

Breaks allow recovery and restore your get-up-and-go. It is important to take regular mini breaks as well as longer breaks.

A five-minute break every hour is of more benefit than working for long periods then taking an hour off. There are various ways to remind you that it is time to take a break.

❏   Install activity-monitoring software. There are a number on the market, like:

  ▪ *RSIGuard* (35), a modern sophisticated software suite as discussed in Chapter 12

  ▪ *Chequers Software* (37). This can be downloaded from the Internet for personal and non-profit use

  ▪ *WorkPace* (38), a sophisticated package for RSI prevention and rehabilitation, offers a trial version that can be downloaded from the Internet

- *ScreamSaver* (39) offers a free 30-day trial. It allows for easy adaptation for individual needs (se Chapter 12)

❑ Set an alarm clock or timer on the far side of the room!

❑ Get up and take your message to a colleague rather than email

❑ Stand up! Look out of the window while you think, or read standing up

❑ Do some stretches or move to music

❑ Make sure you take your lunch and tea break.

Case Study 3   Overwork ends career

With a first class honours degree, Miss McNeil was a highly paid consultant. Her team visited clients to evaluate their management and communication. Conditions were often unsuitable for laptop use. Also, she did not take adequate breaks, often working 12-14 hours a day for 6 or 7 days a week.

Within 9 months, Miss McNeil had pain in her hands and forearms that faded over weekends. After a few months, pain was constant and interfered with her sleep. She went to the Accident and Emergency Department when the pain was intolerable and was told to take aspirin. Working was difficult. At home she needed help with cooking, opening doors etc and could not drive. Her GP signed her off and referred her to a rheumatologist who diagnosed non-specific pain syndrome.

Her company was supportive and changed her task to interviewing job applicants. She found this boring and not relevant to the dynamic career she'd planned. She did not improve. Then the firm paid for private hospital treatment and after a week she became almost pain free - until she went home. She retired on medical grounds. Pain persisted and moved to her wrists, forearms, upper arms and shoulders. It was worse when she was tired. The best relief was lying down or having a hot bath. A period of cognitive therapy helped her to come to terms with her disability.

Outcome

After a year there was no improvement. She reached a financial settlement with her company. She knew any future job could not involve computers so chose a career as a belly dancer. On a tour of the Middle East she met and married a Saudi Prince. They have 2 children and plenty of help in the home. She is still limited in the use of her hands.

For full report see (40)

14. Keep fit

Regular exercise – even the most gentle – is essential if you are to keep fit, especially in the static world of computing.

If you have developed RSI, improving your general fitness will certainly improve your chances of maximum recovery!

When you hurt the temptation is to curl up and hibernate but this will only make things worse. So keep mobile! You need to work on improving your muscle tone and circulation.

If exercise is not part of your routine begin now! It is never too late. Start gently, and under medical guidance, if you already have RSI. You may want to start with something very gentle like Kalenetics, or a set of appropriate gentle movements. Walking in the fresh air has added benefits.

If you want a more structured program you may want to use a gym or start swimming under guidance.

If you are fit you are more likely to 'beat the mouse!'

General fitness is influenced by your diet. Recent findings on the rehabilitation of RSI sufferers highlight the significance of good nutrition in building up the immune system (41).

15. Work in a healthy environment

Almost all computer work is done sitting down and often for long periods. Pay attention to how you sit, to the equipment, and take breaks and exercise.

Be comfortable. Work in an unstressed body position. You need the right setup for you. But even the best setup in the world won't make a significant difference if you don't take care of yourself.

Your upper body should be balanced and your muscles under the least possible tension. Every person is unique with different body proportions. For example the upper arm length varies considerably.

It is not always easy to know whether you are sitting with the 'right' posture. You may need someone with ergonomic knowledge to assess you and help you to begin to replace old damaging habits with healthy ones.

16. Workstation setup fit for you

The **checklists** that follow are inspired and adapted from from MIT's website (2).

Answering the questions below will help you to assess how you work, your posture, and your workstation setup.

If you answer 'no' or are unsure of your answers to any of the questions, take corrective action to avoid the risk of developing RSI.

For more information contact your local Health and Safety Office or an organisation like the HSE (3), UK RSI Association (8) (hosted by Keytools (9)), or visit a website like MIT's (2). For suitable products consult firms like Posturite UK (42), Keytools (9), etc.

17. Check your posture

The human body is designed for movement. Yet in this technological age we spend hours sitting slouching over computers or transfixed in front of the television. Poor posture, coupled with lengthy static sessions is a major contributor to RSI. Good posture is so important that it is worth spending some time on.

What is good posture?
This includes balance and movement! Your body has a natural alignment when it is under least stress. Your head and upper-body should balance on your mid-body and lower back. When this is the case you don't use muscle tension to hold things in place. Good posture does not mean holding one position for a long time. Rather the key is harmony of movement and then your muscles will not fatigue easily.

'With good posture natural body alignment is supported by gravity; with poor posture, gravity pulls down on whatever is out of alignment, such as a forward head, slumped shoulders or a curved back.' (43) This can become cyclical and lead to worsening posture and then to problems like pinched nerves, herniated disks and joints with reduced movement.

The Alexander Technique is a method that helps with understanding about and gaining and maintaining good balance and good posture (Chapter 42). If you cultivate the technique you will have a tool to help you manage your posture for life.

There are other helpful methods and some are described in Chapter 42.

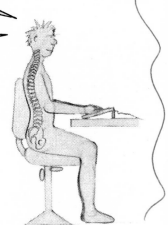

*This is a **GOOD** posture:*
Low stress and balanced

When you begin a session at a computer you may start out with good intentions in a good posture. But as you sit working for long periods with no breaks the muscles that hold up your head, shoulders and arms grow tired and lose their strength.

As neck and shoulders fatigue your shoulders roll forward. You slouch and your front neck muscles tug on the area where the nerves and blood vessels to your arms pass out between the first rib and collarbone (called the thoracic outlet).

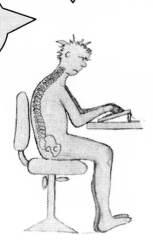

***Avoid this BAD** posture:*
High stress and slouching

Easier said than done!
If you spend long periods at your computer gravity wins.

Your shoulders also collapse over your armpits pressing on a complex intersection of all the nerves of the arm (the brachial plexus). Pressure on the blood vessels reduces the blood flow to the arms. Trouble may follow as waste product removal through muscle metabolism is inhibited.

Overworked muscles become inflamed and often cut off nerves and blood flow. For more on the complexity and vulnerability of nerve pathways in the hands, arm, neck etc. when over exposed to lengthy activity see (43) and Chapter 39.

Fatigue in the large shoulder and neck muscles causes the forearm and hand muscles to overwork. These small bands of muscles, which drive the fingers, are probably already overloaded due to repetitive typing.

The most blatant typing offences are bending the wrists up (dorsiflexion),

and bending the wrists out (Ulnar deviation).

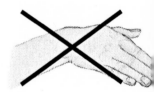

These positions overwork the small muscle bands of the forearm as you reach with fingertips instead of moving the whole arm.

As you lose stamina you may rest your hands on the edge of the work surface. Pressure on the wrist can cause reduced blood flow through the ulnar artery and pinch the ulnar nerve going to the fingers. The ulnar nerve controls movement and sensation in the little finger and the ring finger (See Chapter 39) .

For a more detailed explanation on good and bad postural habits see (43).

Check your own working habits and make necessary changes.

❑ **Feet**: Are your feet resting fully and firmly on the floor or footrest?

❑ **Knees**: Are your knees bent at approximately right angles?

❑ **Thighs:** Are your thighs supported and parallel to the floor, or tilting slightly forwards, so the chair does not put pressure on the back of your thighs?

❑ **Upper body**: Is your upper body straight and your lower back firmly supported by the chair backrest?

❑ **Arms:** Are your arms hanging straight down at your sides loosely from your shoulders?

❑ **Elbows**: Are your elbows at your side and at right angles?

❑ **Forearms**: Are your forearms parallel to the floor as you work on the keyboard and mouse?

❑ **Wrists:** Are your wrists straight, neither bent up or down nor to the left or right?

Do your wrists lean on anything while you are typing or using the mouse? While it is alright to lean on your wrists while resting it could be harmful to you to do so when actively using the mouse or typing.

❑ **Head**: Is your head looking straight forward or with only a slight downward tilt?

Case Study 4   Novelist defeats RSI threat

A novelist's worst nightmare came true.

As Sophie was finishing her third novel, against a tight deadline, suddenly her hands seized up. The pain made her want to scream but that was nothing compared to the panic she felt. A writer just can't function without a pen, or typing.

Sophie had written for years and never felt a twinge. Now she had pains in her hands, arms and elbows, and her back began to stiffen. She saw her GP who referred her to a consultant physiotherapist.

Everything stemmed from Sophie's bad posture, nerves were being trapped and she was using the wrong muscles.

Sophie reviewed her work setup and invested in a bigger mouse, an adjustable chair, a hydraulic lift desk, etc. and tried voice recognition software - that did not suit her. She took up Pilates. It helped her back.

Eventually Sophie started typing again, a little at a time. She stopped at the slightest tingling, took breaks and tried to sit up straight.

After about 3 months she was back at work more or less full time and still is, a year later.

(For full article see (44))

18. Use a suitable chair

How you sit is just as important as the computer you use. Often poor seating arrangements are a major factor in developing RSI. A chair that doesn't give you the support you need is a recipe for developing shoulder and neck fatigue – a prelude to getting RSI.

Make sure your chair provides you with the support you need to sit comfortably and in a healthy way. There are top of the range as well as more affordable chair solutions. In either case ask:

❑ Can you adjust your chair to make the seat the right height for you?

❑ Does your seat have a forward tilt mechanism?

❑ If your chair is adjustable, do you know how to adjust it?

❑ Does the backrest give firm support on your lower back?

❑ Is the front edge of the seat rounded to avoid pressure on the back of your thighs?

❑ Does the chair have castors so that it rolls easily?

❑ Do you have a footrest, if you need one?

❑ If your chair is not height adjustable can you improvise so that it is the right height?

Affordable solutions

You do not need to break the bank in order to sit comfortably. There are ways to improvise. Use cushions, backrests, seat wedges etc (to provide a forward tilt and so that you are seated at the right height). Ready made back rolls, backrests and wedges can be bought from firms like Posturite UK (42).

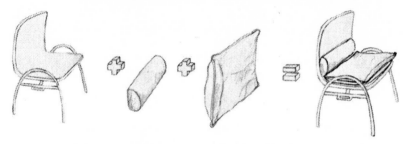

Other items that may be of use include:

Armrests
If used, they should be at the right height for you, and preferably padded, not hard. Do not rest on the armrest when typing or mousing.

Wrist rests
Wrist rests are optional but may do more harm than good if they are used while typing or mousing. When actively using a computer your wrists should be free to move. They *should not* lean on any surface including wrist rests as this can restrict the blood flow.

Footrest
Any solid or rocking platform may be used if needed.

Software that 'clicks' for you
Clicking the mouse repeatedly may become painful. There are products on the market that will 'click' for you such as ActiveClick (45) and RSIGuard (35).

19. The right keyboard for you

Where possible make sure the keyboard (and other equipment you use) suits you rather than trying to adapt to equipment that doesn't.

Ask these questions to help you adjust your existing keyboard or change for one more suitable:

❑   Is the keyboard detached from the monitor?

❑   Can the keyboard height be adjusted to suit you?

❑   Is the keyboard at the right height so that your elbows are at your sides, forearms parallel to the floor, and your wrists are straight?

❑   Is the keyboard parallel to the floor?

❑   Is the keyboard on a foam pad to soften the impact of your fingers on the keys?

❑   Do the keys give audible feedback to stop you from pressing too hard?

❑   Can your fingers reach the shift and function keys?

Ergonomic keyboards

Ergonomic alternatives to the standard keyboard (and mouse) are on the market. When using a traditional keyboard your wrists are twisted at 12 degrees from the safest position – one of the causes of wrist problems.

The range of alternatives is growing. These include cord free, angle adjustable and split keyboards. You can find examples at Microsoft (7 and 46), Keytools (9) and Maltron (47).

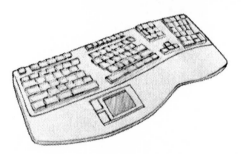

The designers of Maltron keyboards claim that their keyboard range enables RSI sufferers and people with special needs to use a computer without strain or injury and that their keyboards have enabled numerous people with RSI to return to work.

Note – some split keyboards still keeps wrists angled at 5 degrees from the optimum.

There is no one universal perfect solution. The best you can do is to try out various keyboards to find the one that suits you.

Whatever keyboard you use, you need to take frequent breaks. Overuse can have devastating consequences.

20. Your mouse

The mouse is by far the most common non-keyboard input device used with desk computers and laptops. Software has become mouse-driven and 30% of the time spent using a keyboard involves the mouse.

Usually the mouse is to the side of the keyboard and using it in this position causes additional strain on the neck and shoulder muscles. The wider the keyboard, the greater the stretch and stress on your muscles.

Clicking and holding the mouse can add strain. Global evidence shows that it contributes significantly towards musculoskeletal problems appearing as pain or discomfort in the lower back, neck, shoulders, wrists and hands. This is giving rise to international concern.

Microsoft (7) recognised this early on. For example, their *Getting Started guides* for pointing devices include warnings like this (though often in the small print).

Many attempts are made to reduce the physiological effects of using the mouse. For example a small mouse enclosed in a larger casing to ease the hand grip on a small object is called a mouse-topper.

Use of the keyboard or mouse may be linked to serious injuries or disorders.

If you experience symptoms such as recurring or persistent discomfort, pain, throbbing, burning sensation or stiffness in your shoulder, neck, arms or hands

DO NOT IGNORE THESE WARNING SIGNS; PROMPTLY SEE A QUALIFIED HEALTH PROFESSIONAL.

Mice are designed in all shapes and sizes – small and big, some moulded to the shape of a hand, others include a scroll wheel, and the newest breeds are wireless.

71

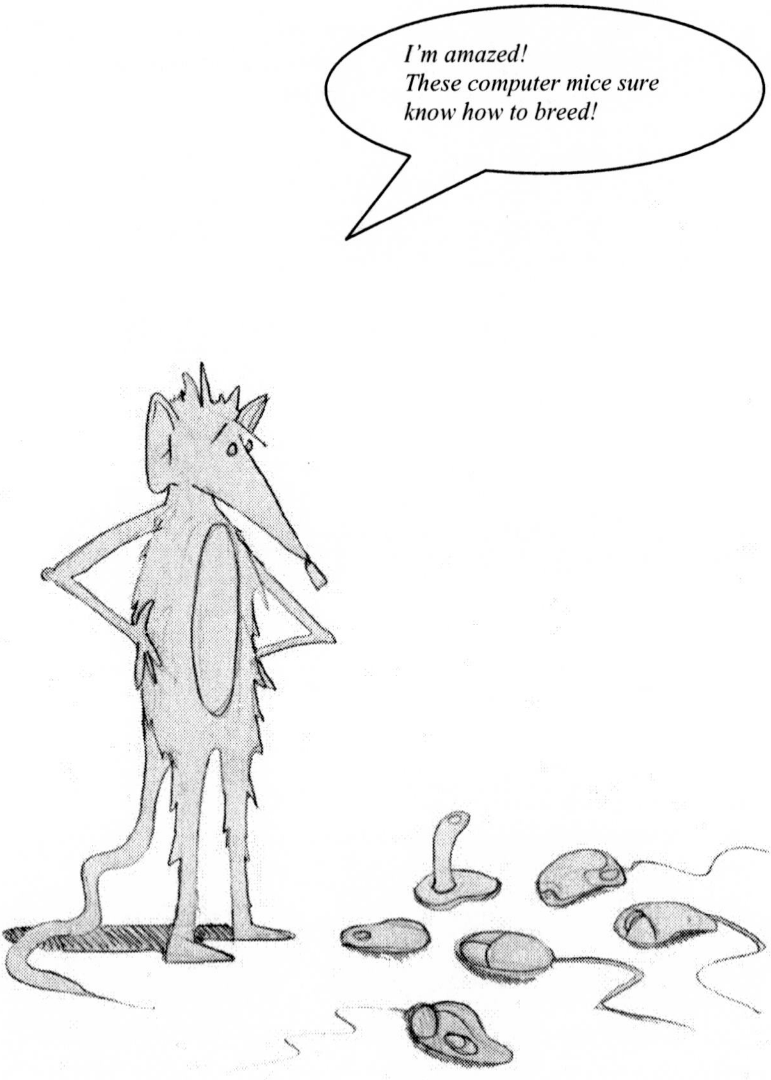
I'm amazed!
These computer mice sure
know how to breed!

Choosing your mouse or mice
It is important to use the mouse that suits you best. Every person is different and there is no universal mouse that suits everyone. There is a great variety to choose from and no shortage of companies selling these. If possible get help choosing to ensure the best ergonomic solution for you.

Recently, Keytools (9) recommended I use two different mice with my laptop and alternate using these. The reason behind this was that different muscles are used in operating each, helping to eliminate repetition and thus playing a part in avoiding RSI.

I took this advice and find swapping between using a touch pad, embedded in and central to my laptop, and a Microsoft wireless mouse, much more comfortable, especially on long jobs. In addition I have added one more tool for inputting data – Dragon Naturally Speaking version 8 (See Chapter 26). This enables me to speak to my computer where appropriate, but to use the keyboard or mouse when more suitable.

Try before you buy when choosing a new mouse
Some suppliers allow you to test out mice before paying for one in the store. If you can't find what you need nearby, look on the Internet and order what seems to be the best fit for you. Before ordering, ensure you can return your mouse if it does not suit you.

Some companies offer training materials and good support. In the UK these include Keytools (9), Posturite (42), and Osmond (48). There are numerous international companies, including Targus (49).

These questions help you decide on the right mouse:

- ❑ Is your mouse positioned so you can avoid reaching or stretching when you are using it?

- ❑ Is it comfortable and easy to operate?

- ❑ Is the size suitable for your hand?

- ❑ Is its movement smooth?

- ❑ Does it provide good control and precision?

- ❑ Is it sufficiently responsive and speedy?

- ❑ Is the mouse at the right height so you can move it comfortably with your arm parallel to the floor and wrist straight, not tilting up or down?

'Breeds' of mice

I was intrigued to discover around 40 different mice on offer on Keytools site (9) alone! Breeds include:

- ❑ The **Anir Vertical Mouse** – allows you to hold your hand in a natural position (50)

- ❑ **The ordinary Mouse**

- ❑ **The Marble Mouse** – suited for left or right handed people, has the precision of a trackball

- ❑ **Squeaky Mouse** – a touch-sensitive mouse that prompts the computer to squeak when you press too hard (51)

❑ **The Mouse Bean** – not a mouse but a 'kidney bean' shaped extension to attach to an ordinary mouse providing support and comfort

❑ **Cordless / wireless Mouse.** Several options – enables you to work more flexibly

❑ **The MouseTrapper** – a most unusual and versatile ergonomic mouse. This mechanical device fits over a standard keyboard. The mouse is 'trapped' in a cradle (1) and activated by a scroll bar (2) and the flip keys (3). Your hands operate in a more natural position, with less stress, and hence the MouseTrapper helps to relieve and prevent RSI. There is the option of removing the mouse from its cradle and using it conventionally. For a free trial see (52).

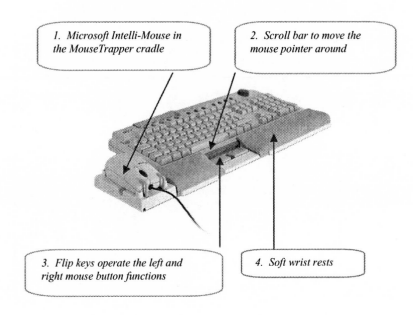

1. Microsoft Intelli-Mouse in the MouseTrapper cradle

2. Scroll bar to move the mouse pointer around

3. Flip keys operate the left and right mouse button functions

4. Soft wrist rests

Adapted from Posturite (42)

Case Study 5   Mouse ends typist's career

Since 1987 Mrs Green had worked for an electrical wholesaler. She had no problems with her hands and arms until annual stocktaking in 1998 when she was 34.

At the end of a working week she was asked to stock take over the weekend. It took her 20 hours in poor conditions. Then she was told some data she'd been given was false and asked to repeat the job the next weekend. This she did. Astonishingly she was asked to do the work a third time due to more data errors. As she finished she was aware of pain and swelling in her wrists but continued to work, and for the next 3 months survived by taking painkillers.

Her GP diagnosed tennis elbow and tenosynovitis, prescribed anti-inflammatory drugs and told her to take a month's sick leave. Nothing improved but she needed the money so returned to work. Over the next year she got worse. When it was too painful to use the mouse in her right hand she used it with her left. By October 1999 she was no longer able to use a computer and was put off work. In January 2000 she was made redundant and has not worked since. A rheumatologist diagnosed RSI. She had regular physiotherapy and 3 local steroid injections.

Outcome
By 2001 she'd improved but was very limited in tasks like cooking, driving, turning knobs or carrying shopping.
Mrs Green, a conscientious, hardworking person who responds to a challenge, paid the price for her dedication. She is a classic example of the type of person who develops RSI!

All agreed her problem was caused by work and she received £36,000 compensation, settled out of court.

For full report see (53)

76

My advice is:
Try before you buy.

The cordless mouse is very popular. ***But*** *I don't think I'd look good, or function well, without my balancing tail!*

The UK Health and Safety Executive has useful information on using a mouse safely (54).

Other devices and software that may help
There are several alternative non-keyboard input devices available if a mouse does not suit you. These include trackballs, joysticks, touch-pads and touch-screens.

Warning
Although it is worth trying out different devices to find those that suit you best, beware of running from one device to another! You can end up shifting your RSI discomfort to a different part.

21. Use keyboard shortcuts

Used regularly, keyboard shortcuts can greatly reduce the mouse-strain on your hands, arms etc. Those given here are for Windows and a subset of what you can find on the Microsoft support website – see (55).

Windows system key combinations

F1:	Help
CTRL+ESC:	Open **Start** menu
ALT+TAB:	Switch between open programs
ALT+F4:	Quit program
SHIFT+DELETE:	Delete item permanently

Windows program key combinations

CTRL+C:	Copy
CTRL+X:	Cut
CTRL+V:	Paste
CTRL+Z:	Undo
CTRL+B:	Bold
CTRL+U:	Underline
CTRL+I:	Italic

General keyboard-only commands

F10:	Activates menu bar options
SHIFT+F10	Opens a shortcut menu for the selected item (this is the same as right-clicking an object)
CTRL+ESC or ESC	Selects the **Start** button (press TAB to select the taskbar, or press SHIFT+F10 for a context menu)

The monitor / screen

A workstation must be placed so that there is no direct glare or reflections on the screen. If necessary, use a window blind to cut out the reflected light. An anti-glare device can be attached to your screen. Every effort must be made to allow for comfortable working and to avoid eyestrain.

Use this checklist

❑ Is the monitor at the proper viewing distance for you? (Usually 40-60 centimetres from your eyes.)

❑ If the screen is small, is the top of the screen at eye level? If the screen is large, is the centre of the screen at eye level?

❑ Is the monitor directly in front of you, rather than off to the side?

❑ Can the monitor height be adjusted?

❑   Do you have a copy stand or document holder to hold your papers? If so, is it at the same height and distance from you as the screen?

❑   If necessary do you have an anti- glare device attached to your screen?

22.   Laptop computers

Increasingly laptops are used as part of normal work. They are particularly useful because they are portable, enabling you to work wherever you are.

Originally laptops were 'intended for occasional, short-term use rather than continuous use' (54). Now they are becoming increasingly powerful and often used instead of a PC. 'It is predicted that by 2007, 50% of all PC users will be using a laptop – and often as their primary PC' (49).

Laptops are frequently used on unsuitable surfaces – for example, in trains, hotel rooms or libraries, with limited legroom, poor seating and bad lighting, and where it is difficult to have the screen at the right height.

Laptop use requires a new approach to comfort, well-being and efficiency.

Hazards associated with the use of laptops

Most laptops have the screen attached to the keyboard. This is not ergonomically friendly!

I'm told this a bad position for working.
But what can I do?
It is all I've got and I've got to work!

If no modification is made when a using a laptop it will force you to work in an unhealthy position. Gravity pulls down causing unnecessary strain on the muscles supporting your head, neck, shoulders and back. Over time this could have a detrimental effect on your wellbeing.

The usual options are

❏ **Raise your laptop** so that the screen is at the right height, plug in and *work on a separate keyboard.* You can do this by acquiring a *laptop riser.* These fold flat, are portable and are widely available. Your laptop keyboard then doubles as a document stand.

If you prefer, and at no additional expense, you can stand your laptop on pile of books and work in a relaxed position!

❏ **Use a second screen** at the right height. A function button enables you to switch between the laptop screen and the second screen

❏ **Use a separate mouse** if you find the touchpad too restricting. By using a mouse *and* touchpad you will be using different sets of muscles thus avoiding some repetition

82

Carrying a laptop (some weigh over 5 kilograms) for long periods, with other luggage, also exposes you to the risk of musculoskeletal problems associated with the back, neck and head. Where possible use a laptop rucksack.

Checklist for safe laptop use:

❑ Do you create a safe work environment wherever you use your laptop?

❑ Is your screen large enough? If not, do you plug in a larger one and raise it to the right height?

❑ Can you plug your laptop into a docking station, effectively converting your laptop to a desktop computer?

❑ Do you adjust the magnification on the screen so your laptop is easy to read without squinting or slouching forwards?

❑ Whilst travelling, does the pointing device (trackball, button or whatever) cope with movement and vibration?

❑ Have you read the previous chapters in this section? There you will find guidelines on good practice that apply equally to using laptops.

Case Study 6   Journalist quits due to RSI

At 25, Meg enjoyed her work for a London's women's weekly reporting on fashion in Britain and abroad. Her office and workstation were well set up. Her workload would peak before a magazine went to press and then she could take 3 days off. On trips away she carried her laptop over her shoulder and used it for hours on trains, planes and in hotel rooms. She thought the aches she felt at times in her shoulders and back were due to carrying her laptop and overnight bag.

As she became more successful she'd often miss lunch and breaks, working on computers up to 12 hours a day. Then one time after visiting Paris fashion shows she got 'cramps' in her right hand. She'd stop work and flex her arms, hands and fingers but soon had pain in both hands, her back, and her shoulders. She failed to take these symptoms seriously. Gradually they became persistent and severe. After 3 years, pain interfered with her sleep, and she'd miss deadlines. Her boss was unsympathetic and did not take her doctor's advice on job rotation, but gave her a month's sick leave. Meg felt bad as it put pressure on her colleagues. To keep going on return to work she took painkillers but got worse. 'Writers' cramp' due to computer overuse was diagnosed by a rheumatologist.

Outcome

By 30 things were very difficult for Meg – constant pain affected her total life. Pain management classes at St Thomas' Hospital, London, helped her to come to terms with her disability. She quit the job she loved, was bored, and lived on unemployment benefit. Her firm's lawyer, while not accepting liability, gave her a settlement of £83,000 based on loss of earnings, and the understanding she would return to university to complete a teacher's training course, and that her resultant salary would be less than a journalist's.

For full report see (56)

84

23. Work area

❑ Does the desk have a lower surface for the keyboard and higher surface for the monitor, either built-in or attached?

(Alternatively, can you adjust your chair to enable you to work in an ergonomic position – i.e. sitting comfortably, feet on the floor, arms parallel to the floor, hands not bent or straining outwards, screen at an easy height so your eyes are looking straight ahead approximately at the middle of the screen?)

❑ Do you use a document holder when you are reading pages, at the same height as the screen, while you type? This saves you bending your neck awkwardly while you are working.

❑ Are you able to use the phone without having to squeeze the receiver with your shoulder while you type? Consider using a headset instead of the traditional handset. If you use a voice-activated system, do you know that a switch is available that allows use both of the phone and the voice-activated system?

❑ Can you reach the keyboard and mouse comfortably without straining forwards?

❑ Is the area under your desk clear to give you comfortable legroom?

❑ Do you use a footrest if your feet do not rest comfortably on the floor?

❑   Is there enough space to put the equipment and other materials at the proper distance without crowding?

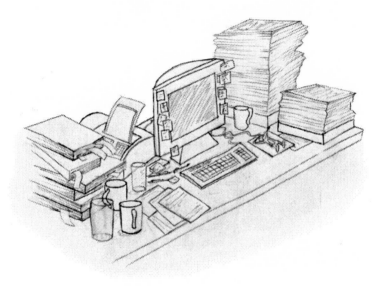

❑   Are standing counters available, if appropriate, so you can alternate sitting and standing while doing computer work?

24. Vision

Have you had your eyesight checked within the last year? If not, make an appointment. It is pointless sorting out other aspects to enable you to work ergonomically if you have to strain your eyes in order to see the monitor clearly. It is possible you may need special glasses to use when looking at a computer screen.

When using a computer, your eyes are focused at a fixed distance. Researchers have shown that poor eyesight can develop due to long hours of close work.

As a step towards avoiding this fixed focus hang a large mirror directly behind your monitor, preferably a wider one than in this picture! As you work pause frequently, look into the mirror and the 'distant' room behind you. This provides your eyes with exercise.

Otherwise make a conscious effort to look up from your screen frequently and fix your gaze on a more distant object – for example look out of a window or at the other side of the room.

A simple exercise to refresh the circulation of the eyeball, suggested by an optician, is to pause frequently to blink in this way:

> look up – blink
> look down – blink
> look right – blink
> look left – blink.

25. Use your voice

Use your voice and save your hands! It can be more
relaxing than tapping away at the keyboard in a static
position. For the average user dictating long documents
it can be a lot quicker than typing. Voice recognition
software can benefit anyone.

You can use your voice to create written documents, e-
mails, search the web, keep track of your finances,
manipulate graphics, etc.

> *If RSI is threatening, or is already a reality, using
> your voice could play a large part in enabling you to
> keep working and hold down your job.*

Voice recognition software, inadequate until the late
nineties, has improved dramatically. Numerous systems
are on the market. Amongst the best known are the
IBM Via Voice and Dragon Naturally Speaking ranges.
Dragon Naturally Speaking, Version 8 Professional (12)
provides the opportunity to work in different languages,
assists with translation etc.

The professional editions let you work in any Windows
application – read, or listen to incoming email or other
documents being read aloud, or dictate directly into
Windows   applications   like   Microsoft   Word,
PowerPoint, Spreadsheets and Access. If your need is
more basic buy the standard or home versions.

Good systems allow you to speak naturally (continuous
speech recognition) and train software to know your
style, introduce new words to the vocabulary, control
the mouse with your voice, and correct and edit.

A mobile addition to the voice recognition world is the *digital voice recorder*. This enables you to dictate while you are away from your computer and download your piece when you are back at base.

However good your voice recognition system, it does require some effort from you to make it work well. As you use the system it learns about your voice and pronunciation. When you use words the system doesn't know, it will write what it thinks it hears. You then have the chance to correct the mistake.

Voice recognition software is constantly improving. Check the Internet or a specialist speech recognition firm to find the version that best suits your need. A half day's good training can give you a flying start.

26. Mobile phones and texting

The popularity of mobile phones and text messaging (*texting* or *sending a text*) continues to soar and so do the associated RSI consequences (See Case Study 8). As handsets become smaller buttons are closer together and more difficult to use. It is the small fine movements that tend to aggravate more than larger movements.

Did you know?

* *The first text message was sent in December 1992*
* *Since the dawn of the New Millennium texting has grown from a popular craze to an essential communication tool*

In the UK
After the Christmas sales of December 2004, the number of mobile phones in circulation exceeded the size of the UK population (57).
The number of text messages sent continues to rocket:
* *In August 2001 there were over one billion (a first)*
* *In May 2005 the total was 2.63 billion   (58)*
* *June 2006 figures show an increase of 30% on last year's total for the same period   (TEXT.IT see (58))*
The <u>forecast for the year 2005</u> (Mobile Data Association)
   was <u>32 billion text messages</u>   (57)

The UK Chartered Society of Physiotherapy (CSP) points out that 'too much text messaging can result in pain and swelling of the tendons at the base of the thumb and wrist. The thumb is not a very dexterous digit. It is good for grasping but not for repetitive movement' (59).

A mobile is usually held in the palm of the hand with the fingers in a claw-like position. This creates tension in the fingers, up the back of the hand and up the arm to the shoulders and the neck, while the thumb with lightning speed pounds the keyboard. The three components to overuse are:

Frequency
Duration
Intensity

When texting you need to look at how often you repeat the same movement. If you are texting for more than 10-15 minutes at a time, it can lead to problems (59).

How to text safely
Adapted from Chartered Society of Physiotherapists (CSP) and the Mobile Data Association (MDA) (60)

❑ While texting, where possible, support your arm on a chair or table to take the 'load' off your neck and shoulder muscles.

❑ Hold the phone up and facing towards you so you do not have to flex your neck too much as you view the screen

❑ Keep your arms close to your body. Although the weight of the phone may not be great, the load on your arms increases significantly if your arm is stretched out This action puts strain on your neck and shoulder muscles

- Take a break or swap hands often before the onset of any discomfort

- Try to text using both hands to 'spread the load'

- Learn the predictive text feature on your phone. This reduces the number of keystrokes

- If your hand or forearm feels tense or sore,

STOP!

Massage your arm from the wrist to the elbow

- Do relevant exercises as often as possible – for example, three recommended by the CSP and Mobile Data Association:

Recommended exercises

1. Regularly open your fingers and stretch them out

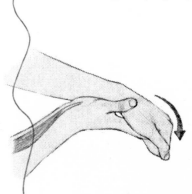

2. Stretch your arm out; rotate your wrist so it is facing upwards. With your other hand pull your palm down towards the floor to feel a stretch over the front of your forearm muscles. Hold for 15 seconds and repeat 2-3 times.

Stretch your arm out; rotate your wrist so it is facing downwards. With your other hand pull your hand back towards your wrist to feel a stretch over the back of your forearm muscles. Hold for 15 seconds and repeat 2-3 times.

27. Get enough rest

When you sleep your batteries recharge and the natural healing processes of your body come into play.

When you do not have enough rest you slouch more easily and unhealthy consequences may follow.

Rest is the best.
You work best
when you are zested!
ZZZ zzz ZZZ zzz ZZZ!

Let your body tell you how much rest you need and make sure you get it on a regular basis.

28. Keep warm while you work

When you are cold your muscles function poorly and the risk of RSI increases. Some people are prone to having cold hands and feet especially when static for long periods.

If you have cold hands, try soaking them in hot water before you start a session on the computer. Rub them together while reading text on the screen or thinking. Another solution is to have a hot water bottle on your lap and rest your hands on it whenever your hands are not active on the computer.

Warm-up exercises and keeping an acceptable temperature in your working environment will also help.

D. Children beware!

29. The Information Superhighway

Around the globe children from an early age are spending more and more time using the products of the microchip age. They are quick to sample the thrills and benefits of the hi-tech inventions, be it playing for long hours uninterrupted on computer games, online gaming, communicating via email, texting on the latest mobile phone, or surfing the Net for fun or for school projects.

Peer group pressure ensures an increase in the number of children communicating in these ways.

'At the moment one in four children has a computer in their bedrooms. This development is likely to increase. When parents upgrade their computers they often pass the old ones to their to children' (61).

Text messaging
There is a phenomenal increase in **text messaging** (see Chapter 27, (58)). In 2005 when the UK GCSE results were announced 79 million text messages were sent that evening. (**General Certificate of Secondary Education** is taken at around age 16.)

If you watch a young person texting you will notice the lightning speed at which the thumbs and index fingers pound the keypads of these ever-smaller mobile phones.

Messages are usually created using the thumb and index finger of the dominant hand. 'It is already clinically recognised that this technique can lead to local soft-tissue injury. Poor posture whilst texting – often standing with arms elevated – can lead to problems in the cervical and thoracic spine' (61). As the movements are small they do not cause the blood to circulate and so fresh oxygen supplies are denied and toxins are not removed.

Online gaming
This is progressively captivating more and more teens – especially boys. Games can be played with anyone around the world who has access to the Internet. There are global concerns that addiction to the captivating world of the Internet and online gaming brings with it mental, social and physical perils when too much time is spent in front of a computer.

Take one example – an estimated 25 million Chinese play online games. 'In Shanghai 15% of teenagers are addicted to the Internet and to online gaming' (62).

China is taking steps to introduce an 'anti-online game addiction system' as reported in the Financial Times in August 2005. 'This system, which will encourage players to play less by cutting the benefits they gain in online games, is to be implemented by local internet companies' (63). However, by March 2006, 'Seven months after the announcement of the anti-addiction policy, it is still only being tested on a small number of servers operated by the big game companies' (64). Read about this and the ongoing question in the references given and by searching the Internet for *'online gaming'*.

30. Danger signs – children at risk

Research is exposing the danger now facing a computer generation of youngsters. On the basis of medical evidence there is growing concern around the world that intensive and prolonged use of modern technologies, such as XBoxes, mobile phones, computers, online gaming, etc. is putting kids at risk of permanent and painful injuries.

'Experts are beginning to see children of eight and younger with RSI who can't tie their shoelaces or carry their rucksacks. And they are starting to make connections between lifestyle and the threat of long-term disability – a disaster waiting to happen. We are concerned children are damaging themselves early on in life and it's only later on the problems will emerge' (65).

Another aspect causing concern is that school students have to carry all their books in mobile lockers – on their backs in a rucksack or in a carry bag. When the critical weight, of around 8 kilograms is exceeded regularly, a huge extra strain results.

Damage is cumulative and RSI problems develop over time. In the last few years I have met students with problems so severe that some have had to dictate their finals. In the worst cases students have had no option but to give up their course altogether.

31. Games galore

'It is estimated that 25% of boys now spend more than 15 hours a week playing with computer game consoles. There are over 5000 computer games available and the computer game market is starting to overtake the cinema as a source of entertainment' (66).

Games played on X-boxes, Play Stations, Game Cubes, etc. require the rapid and repeated use of a player's thumb and/or fingers. Kids get hooked on a game and play at speed for hours if no boundaries are set. Problems are worst when children use consoles lying down or in other poor postures. Manufacturers aware of the problem give warnings in small print such as:

Health Warning

For your health, rest about 15 minutes for each hour of play. Avoid playing when tired or when suffering from lack of sleep. Play in a brightly lit room and keep as far from the television screen as possible.

Play Station Infogrames © Sony Computers 1993-1999

The next warning came with our son's play station:

Repetitive Motion Injuries and Eyestrain

Playing video games can make your muscles, joints, skin or eyes hurt after a few hours. To avoid these problems
- *avoid excessive play. Parents / guardians should monitor children's play*
- *take a break every hour even if you don't think you need it*
- *when using the stylus do not grip it or press too hard*
- *if your hands, wrists, arms or eyes become tired whilst playing STOP and rest them for several hours*

If you continue to have sore hands etc stop playing and see a doctor.

These warnings are seldom read or observed by players and may not be enough to prevent players developing an RSI if too much time is spent on games.

32. Computers in education

The use of computers in nursery schools is becoming the norm and children as young as three are introduced to them. This is the start of the long haul for most, as they will use computers for the rest of their lives.

Will this add to their well-being?

I think I've got them trapped for life!

Researchers at Cornell University have observed that computers in labs are generally not set up with healthy typing posture in mind. 'A 1999 study by Shawn Oates appeared in the journal *Computers in the Schools* and found "striking misfits" between children and computer workstations.

Typically keyboards and monitors were placed too high. Hunched shoulders, awkward wrist positions, and hyperextended necks were some of the findings' (67).

This situation extends to most libraries, classrooms and homes where frequently kids use computers set up for their parents.

In schools and in higher education the use of computers in higher education increased dramatically. Even though most students will use technology once they have a job, no training is given on how to use computers in ways that best benefit them in the longer term.

For example, little notice is taken of variations in children's heights and body size, like different arm lengths (see Chapter 6). In many schools in the UK the common bucket-style plastic chairs and tables of fixed height are the norm. So kids sit scrunched up, or with their legs dangling above the floor.

This becomes their model and accepted way of working at a computer. Although thousands are spent on equipment, suitable chairs and work areas are more often than not left out of the budget.

The drive to keep up to date with information technology to improve standards and delivery of education is a costly business. Inevitably what will prove even more costly (in pain and in pounds) is the healthcare of children who suffer because vital elements in the equation have been omitted.

The rapid rise in the use of laptops in schools is lauded. The bad news is that these modern tools, with the keyboard attached to the screen, force a damaging posture.

Hours hunched up in front of a laptop may be of short-term advantage but what of the potential long-term ill health effects?

Seldom are time and resources spent on training staff in what constitutes good ergonomics (the science of fitting the equipment to the user and not training the user to meet the demands of the equipment), so that children can learn good habits for life from the outset.

33. Wake-up warnings

Computer-induced RSI is no longer just associated with office workers. Australian research, led by ergonomics specialist Dr Leon Straker, reveals that children are just as prone. He found symptoms in six out of ten who use a keyboard at school and said: 'We are concerned that serious permanent damage may be done to developing bodies by using computers for this much time' (68).

The situation is the same in the UK. Bunny Martin reports: 'When we asked children whether they suffer from early symptoms of RSI, such as pins and needles or other pains, half the class put up their hands' (69).

The press report 'The RSI Generation' concludes: 'If we do not act now we will be faced with a future generation unable to function in the very environment created to make working life easier' (69). What could be worse?

If preventative principles are not taught fast, and applied, we could find ourselves, five to ten years down the line, with a problem of considerable scale (70).

Regrettably, in spite of these loud warnings, children, their parents, and teachers, usually know nothing of the lurking danger. They don't know the bad news that once RSI has become a problem recovery can be very slow and there is no miracle cure. But there is a positive balance to this – the good news that RSI *can* be prevented.

This UK case study of a child of eight with RSI illustrates the reality of these dangers to children.

Case Study 7   RSI prevents child writing

Mary could use a computer at five. By eight she was more skilled than her father. Her parents worked full time and child minders let her play on games consoles uninterrupted for hours. None knew of the dangers of excessive computer and games use.

One August Mary felt pains in her thumbs and index fingers. When she returned to school the pain stopped her from holding a pencil. She could not do her homework, use a knife and fork, or fasten her buttons. A specialist concluded Mary's symptoms were the result of over-use of games consoles and computers.

To help her recover Mary was banned from computers, game consoles, etc. She had to exercise, play outdoors and read more. After three weeks rest, although her hands were still painful, she was allowed to attend lessons but not write. She improved slowly. After two months she was symptom free and allowed to access computers if she did warm-up exercises beforehand, and took regular breaks every fifteen minutes. She was given an adjustable chair and had to play active games. The specialist told her to avoid computer games permanently as they could cause long-term unwanted physical effects. Little is known about these effects in children whose soft tissue and bones are growing

__Positive outcomes__: Mary's parents encouraged her to do her exercises. She used computers at school where regular talks were given by an occupational health nurse to make children aware of the dangers in using modern technology to hands and arms Parents and their child minders were kept informed of these dangers.

(For full report 70))

34. Towards solutions

On national scales, with some exceptions, not a lot is happening right now to swing the balance in favour of preventative action – raising awareness of RSI and creating a healthy computing climate.

But, what are you and I doing? Perhaps you think that you won't be able to achieve very much. Hold on! History is peppered with appalling situations that have come to an end because people at the grassroots took action. None of us can change this situation alone.

However we need to think BIG and start small! Those of us who have had RSI, together with students, parents, educators and people in the health care professions, must take up this opportunity to do something within education, in our own patch, before an RSI avalanche descends on our young people.

Once a groundswell of effort builds up the scale will be tipped to the prevention side, with the chance of eliminating this unnecessary and debilitating scourge.

Here are some pointers for action that could help you decide where to begin. Although focussed mainly on schools, the same principles apply to higher education, the business world, and the sole practitioner. Follow the path that suits.

Pupils and students

❑ Understand what it means to use computers and games in a healthy way – a benefit for the rest of your life

❑ Remember you are unique and have an important contribution to make to this world. What you don't want is to be straddled with a disability that will hold you back. Two sections in this book will help you to focus on the correct ways of doing things:

- Section C: 'How to avoid RSI'
- **The summary on prevention** on the last page
  Copy this and stick it on your mirror!

- Look carefully at the computer provision and working environment at your school, and decide if it meets healthy standards

- If it does not point this out to the staff and ask for changes to be made

- If nothing happens involve your parents and the school governors

- Know the signs, symptoms and early warnings of a developing RSI problem. These could include pains or pins and needles in your hands, wrist, arms, neck or back. Pain is sometimes worst when resting in bed at night

- If you notice any of these for more than a few days see the school nurse, tell your tutor and your parents and see your doctor

- Follow through any recommendations made

- Ask your friends if they have problems

- If you find others with the same concerns, go as a team to discuss this with your head teacher or a senior member of staff

- Make sure something positive happens.

Case Study 8 A-Level student with RSI

Francis, 18

As I was putting the finishing touches to this book a friend, Francis, who was only 4 months from taking his final school exams, phoned to ask for advice. What could he do to prevent the pains he was experiencing when using various forms of technology?

Francis' story

*Two years ago he used to play **computer games** on a regular basis for about an hour a day. Then he noticed he was experiencing pain in his hands and lower arm when and after playing. He very sensibly stopped playing these games altogether.*

*Now he uses a **computer** for his coursework. Using a joystick cases no problem. But most of the time he uses a **mouse** and this does cause him pain.*

*Recently Francis changed his **mobile phone**. This came with a better deal – **more texts** for the same money as he'd paid on his old mobile. He texts for around a half hour at a time sending some 4-5 messages. He mainly uses his right thumb, which has become painful (and more so since he broke it!). Then he switches to using his left thumb or forefinger. He says that the cost factor had previously stopped him from overuse of his mobile. He has seriously reduced his use of text messaging to help him overcome his RSI.*

Francis' concerns

Francis has two main concerns. He wants to know how to avoid developing a serious and debilitating RSI problem. Secondly he is concerned for some of his friends who admit to pain after gaming, computing or texting for a few hours.

What should Francis do?

My response

Remember two things. There are no quick fixes! The most effective way forward is to take charge of your recovery.

*By stopping computer games when your hands and arm hurt, and reducing texting, you did a brilliant thing. You demonstrated that most important ingredient for recovery - the readiness to **change**.*

A bigger challenge lies ahead. You need to understand what is causing your pain and how to overcome it. You must resolve how to use computers and technology in general, so you stay healthy doing it. Sections B and C in my book will point you in the right direction. There are several interrelated points to work on – your habit patterns, balance between work and play (exercise and relaxation), your workstation / work area setup including chair, keyboard, mouse, monitor, laptop etc. Text messaging – do as little as possible. I enclose my (new) chapter on mobile phones and texting. It includes a few exercises suggested by the Mobile Data Association. Try to get a diagnosis through your doctor.

Involve your school in your recovery
*<u>You must tell the relevant staff member about your RSI.</u> He or she should arrange for an ergonomic evaluation of the equipment you use, as well as your workspace, and make recommended changes within school. Hopefully the school will support you as you seek to overcome your RSI. By getting the school involved you will **raise awareness** of the avoidable RSI dangers more likely to occur when*

- *Workstation setup is poor as in most schools in the UK.*
- *Too much time is spent on computers, games, texting etc.*

You know where to find me if you would like to talk again.

Tonia
February 2006

Parents, guardians – Be proactive!

Parents can be a powerful force influencing decisions made on IT in education. If parents join together with the aim of ensuring safe computing practice is taught in school your views could positively influence policy and ensure greater safety for your children.

❑ Be aware! Educate yourself on what makes for healthy computing habits (see Section C)

❑ Check out what is happening at your kids' school. Speak to the IT support staff, head teacher or head of department. Encourage and support the staff

❑ Talk to other parents about RSI risks and see if you can form a support group for your school

❑ Be long-term kind to your kids. Apply high standards at home! Take an interest in their computer games activities and set boundaries on how long they can use these

---

My guidelines for our teenagers are up to 40 minutes a session, with an advised 5-minute break in the middle and at least an hour between sessions. The proviso is that in any one day they should not spend more than 2-3 hours in total on a computer or playing electronic games. The time I allow varies with the intensity and frequency with which buttons are pressed or keyboards pounded, and how long they have spent on computers at school that day. (They understand why they are restricted – perhaps because of extra kitchen duties when my RSI was at its worst!)

Now, with brilliant break software like RSIGuard (35), you can set the boundaries and let the computer do the monitoring.

❑ Breaks – should include frequent mini-breaks of a few seconds to move and stretch, and then 5 minutes for every 20 minutes on the IT device

❑ Keep a check on their posture when working or playing techno games.

Head teachers, staff and governors

Budget constraints in schools imply top of the range solutions are probably quite unrealistic and out of reach. But it is vital that those involved in school organisations and governance should evaluate the state of their computer provision and instruction. And take action!

The good news is that low-cost adjustments (see below) can be made. What is more, if you are quick off the mark your school could lead the way in a Healthy Computing Campaign. You may even attract funding! More importantly your students could be the first to gain in both the short and long term. Consider these pointers in your evaluation:

Healthy Computing Checklist

❑ Does your school tuition plan include instruction on healthy computing habits? If your answer is NO, do you have a plan to educate the staff whose students use computers

❑ Have you reviewed the state of furniture for student/staff IT used, within the last year? (Good design and well placed equipment doesn't have to break the bank.)

❑ Is it possible to position screens at the right height for each person?

Raising the screen on a box, or unwanted books is one option.

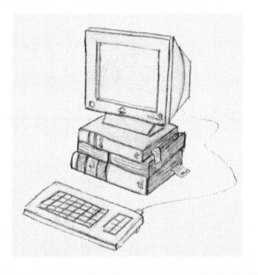

Money saved by buying one computer less *could buy 10 or more height adjustable chairs or many wedges*

❑ Are chairs height-adjustable to enable people of different heights to sit correctly when working at a computer?

❑ Are cushions and seating wedges available?

- Do you set aside part of your budget for developing healthy computing?

- Are footrests provided for people with short legs sitting at an average sized table?

- Are any pointers given to kids about best habits when playing hi tech games?

- Do you know whether students or staff have or have suffered RSI problems?

- Do you know whether any parents have first hand experience of RSI? If YES, do you know if they would be willing to help in your school?

- Are any of your governors in the position to make a contribution towards developing a **Healthy Computing Programme**?

- What action will you take now?

35. Will we adapt in time?

In most schools students work in poor computing conditions, as is the case with adults in offices and homes. Few have the right furniture (or it is usually claimed, the right funding!) to enable healthy computer use, and nor are they aware of what it means to work healthily when computing.

The education of teachers on the elements of a healthy working environment and practice is for the most part missing.

It has become essential to educate teachers and anyone responsible for others at work.

An easy start to educating both teachers and students is to have relevant posters on the wall by every computer.

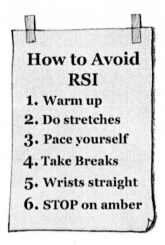

How to Avoid RSI
1. Warm up
2. Do stretches
3. Pace yourself
4. Take Breaks
5. Wrists straight
6. STOP on amber

If we ignore this opportunity to inform and equip young people on how to use modern technology healthily we are going to end up with a generation who are incapacitated before they even get into the workplace.

To be truly effective:

Lessons on good ergonomic practice
must

become part of the core curriculum.

There are more references relating to children in the Further reading section.

E. Digging deeper

Research into RSI

The microchip is young and so is the research into how to avoid the hazards accompanying it. The findings reported here come from a number of countries.

It is not my intention to present a comprehensive overview of existing literature on the subject. That would require effort akin to a doctoral study! Rather I hope this small sample will be helpful to some, eye-opening to others, and provide a flavour of current research that will act as a springboard for further investigation. This is certainly needed.

If you have RSI I trust that it will bring increased understanding and therefore in some way contribute towards your rehabilitation.

36. Other names for RSI

RSI (Repetitive Strain Injury), recognised worldwide, is known by many other names.

Term used	Country
Carpal Tunnel Syndrome (CTS)	USA
Cumulative Trauma Disorders (CTD)	USA
Diffuse RSI	UK
Mouse arm (Muisarm)	Netherlands
Muscle-Tendon Syndrome	Finland
Musculo-Skeletal Injury (MSI)	Canada
Non-Specific foreArm Pain (NSAP)	UK
Occupational Cervico-Brachial Syndrome	Japan
Occupational Overuse Syndrome (OOS)	New Zealand
Repetitive Strain Injury (RSI)	Worldwide
Work-Related Musculoskeletal Disorder (WMSD)	Scandinavia
Work-Related Upper Limb Disorders (WRULD, ULD)	UK
And there are others!	

A questionnaire undertaken by Member States of the European Union in 2000, on terms or definitions used for RSI, shows considerable diversity.

Germany, for example, adopts a strict 'legal' definition (the diseases appearing in the official list of occupational diseases), while others take a broader medico-social view. Various underlying concepts of RSI are used in different Member States, including:

❏ the stress which is the cause (repetitive work/cumulative traumas: tennis elbows, etc.)

❏ the region of the body which is affected (upper limbs/neck, shoulders, etc.)

❏ the disease itself – some (Germany, Denmark and Finland) list well-defined diseases, without employing a common term for them

❏ other countries, such as Sweden, pay more attention to the structures involved (muscles, joints) than to the disease (71).

The report on the questionnaire concludes that the concept of RSI is not uniformly understood.

37. Under the RSI umbrella

RSI is an umbrella term covering many different conditions. The more common are listed in the table below, together with their symptoms.

Don't try to diagnose yourself.
Consult an expert.
Be informed.
It will assist you to
- *understand your condition*
- *help you to help yourself*
- *improve your communication in medical consultations.*

RSI conditions and symptoms

Condition	Symptom
Bursitis	Pain ranging from dull to burning. Possible muscle atrophy.
Carpal tunnel syndrome	Tingling and pain in the hands, primarily in the index and middle fingers and part of the ring finger. Shooting pains up the arm and waking at night due to pain. Possible swelling in the fingers. Grip problems.
De Quervain's disease	Acute pain at the base of the thumb that may radiate to hand or forearm. Grip difficult.

RSI conditions and symptoms continued

Condition	Symptom
Fibromyalgia	Severe aching. Numbness, tingling and swelling. Excessive fatigue. Disturbed sleep patterns.
Ganglion cyst	Visible swelling in the form of a bump or bumps, usually at the back of the hand. Usually not exceptionally painful.
Myofascial pain syndromes	Painful trigger spots that radiate pain when pressed.
Radial tunnel syndrome	Pain on both sides of the forearms. Twisting motion and making a fist difficult. Possible weakness on the top of the hand.
Tendinitis	Dull, aching pain. Feeling of heaviness in the affected area.
Tennis elbow Golfers elbow is similar - Epicondylitis	Radiating pain, felt on the outside or inside of the elbow.
Tenosynovitis	Stiffness. Pain ranging from dull to burning. Possible swelling and crepitus.
Thoracic outlet syndrome	Pain and tingling in neck, shoulders, arms and hands. Coldness and weakness in fingers, hand and forearm. Overhead reaches may cause pain and tingling. Difficult to feel pulse.
Trigger finger	Difficulty making a fist or straightening fingers. May be painful and there may be a cracking or snapping sound when trying to straighten fingers.
Ulnar-nerve irritation	Tingling in hand, primarily in 4th and 5th fingers. May be hard to separate fingers.
Writer's cramp	Involuntary cramping of the hand.

Table adapted (72)

123

38. Medical facets of RSI pain

a. Muscle tension

Research based at Christchurch, New Zealand, concludes that muscle tension is one of the primary causes of RSI. The extract below is adapted from (73).

Diffuse RSI is common especially amongst computer users. This research is the basis of some of the latest medical opinions on the subject.

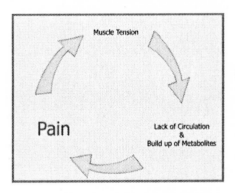

Capillaries passing between muscle fibres supply blood to muscles and tendons. When a tense muscle squeezes on these vessels they collapse and slow the flow of blood, which stops completely when the muscle exerts 50% of its full power.

For brief periods the muscle copes by using stored reserves of energy. Once the reserve is used up acid wastes build up in the muscle (lactic acid). This causes pain and fatigue in the muscle and may cause adjacent muscles to tense up in sympathy. A self-sustaining pain cycle can develop that fluctuates in intensity, from mild to intolerable. The pain can also migrate from one part of the affected limb to another.

If muscles become hypersensitive relatively low levels of activity can cause pain, and tender points known as myofascial trigger points may develop. When there is an inadequate blood supply to nerves numbness and tingling may result. Although factors such as repetition and vibration contribute towards localised conditions such as tendinitis muscle tension is currently regarded as one of the primary causes of RSI.

These mechanisms help to explain why micropauses together with longer breaks are so critical and effective in the treatment and prevention of RSI. In muscles that are regularly refreshed the build up of waste products and fatigue is prevented. *(RSIGuard (35) has inbuilt micropauses called ForgetMeNot MicroBreaks.)*

How RSI becomes a chronic condition
'In the worst cases diffuse RSI can develop into a chronic condition, illustrated by the diagram below.

A number of the physiological and neurological dysfunctions – combined with a loss of muscle tone and physical fitness can result in the seemingly permanent disability, one with similarities to fibromyalgia.' (73)

The mechanisms behind this are not well understood but it appears that recovery and rehabilitation is possible (73).

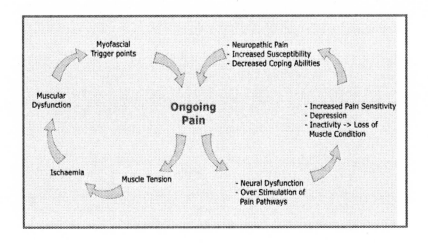

b. Vascular basis

Research at Cardiff, UK, shows that RSI pain is related to an abnormal vascular response to exercise, starving the working muscle of its blood supply (74).

Normally when a muscle starts exercising, the blood supply into the working muscle increases. These findings are that in patients with diffuse RSI the opposite occurs. 'The radial artery at the wrist constricts rather than expands and hence the working muscle is increasingly starved of blood, causing the painful condition known as claudication. This explains the increasing pain patients experience when they work continuously but are otherwise normal healthy people'.

c. Nerve damage

University College London (UCL) research demonstrates forearm pain is associated with median nerve compression in the carpal tunnel (75).

'Magnetic resonance scans on patients with non-specific arm pain (RSI) show reduced median-nerve movement in the carpal tunnel, suggesting that this common condition may involve nerve entrapment' (76).

Rheumatologists studying work-related forearm pain have recently reported that sufferers have abnormally constricted radial arteries and their arteries fail to vasodilate with exercise (77, 78).

London scientists report 'that they use scanning devices to map the way a key nerve moves when healthy people flex their fingers and found that it moves a great deal less for those musicians, keyboard operators and assembly line workers who complained of chronic pain in the hand, wrist or forearm' (79, 80).

'The median nerve runs down the forearm onto the fingers through an arch of bone called the carpal tunnel: so do the tendons needed to grip and flex the fingers.

The median nerve is sheathed in a slippery substance, which helps it move out of the way as the tendons move. When it does not move, the research implies, the trouble begins ' (79).

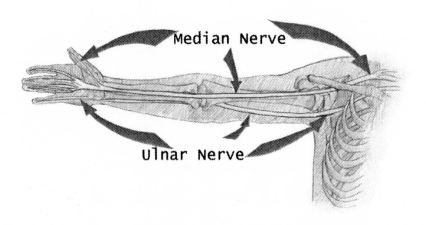

The median nerve extends to the thumb, two adjacent fingers, and part of the next finger (in most people), and controls sensation and movement. The ulnar nerve extends to the little finger and (usually) part of the adjoining finger. The median and ulnar nerves have similar pathways until they reach the back of the arm where the ulnar nerve goes through the 'funny bone' groove. It lies closer to the surface than the median.

There are several places where nerves can be trapped in your arm. One is your wrist when you rest it on the work surface.

Something of the intertwined complexity of the nerve pathways is illustrated at (80) where you will find illuminating illustrations.

d. Mechanical and psychological factors

A study (81) emphasises that the causes of forearm pain are multifactorial. It confirms the relation between work-related repetitive movements and the onset of forearm pain. Levels of psychological distress and work-related psychosocial experiences can predict the onset of symptoms.

The report conclusions are that 'Psychological distress, aspects of illness behaviour, and other somatic symptoms are important predictors of onset of forearm pain in addition to work-related psychosocial and mechanical factors.'

39. Your body

If you understand even the basics of how your body works, how intricate and integrated it is, and how one body system depends on and is supported by the other systems, you have already taken a step onto the ladder of learning how to prevent RSI.

Books, with varying emphasis, that I have found to be particularly enlightening include:

Fearfully and Wonderfully Made (36)
Understanding and Treating RSI (Chapter 3) (11)
BODY: An amazing Tour of Human Anatomy (82)

The latter provides an incredible tour of the human body. The 3D pictures in the book and on the CD were developed from actual body scans. These reveal the astonishing goings on under your skin and what makes you tick. In relation to RSI prevention you may care to study the chapers on hand, wrist, elbow, back and head. These show the incredible complexity and dexterity that enable us to work and that most of us take for granted as we sit hour after hour pouring over our computers.

40. Posture, movement and ergonomics

Ergonomics – The study of human capabilities in relation to their work demands. The word 'Ergonomics' comes from the Greek – 'ergon', meaning work and 'nomoi', meaning natural laws. Work should be fitted to the person rather than the person to the work. Workstation ergonomics means ensuring working in the healthiest position.

In the words of Dr Paul MacLoughlin, Consultant in Occupational Medicine: 'The ergonomic approach is to take account of human needs, requirements and limitations in the design of products, equipment, facilities, procedures and environments. Its aim is to ensure efficiency, safety, ease of use, as acceptable to the user' (83).

The ergonomics4schools site adds an amusing slant:

'Ever tried to eat soup with a fork?
It's not easy, is it? Well, ergonomics is about changing all that! We don't mean making it easy to eat soup with a fork, we mean giving you the right tools for the job. Ergonomics is about making your life simpler and safer by taking account of human characteristics when we design things.' (84)

Movement – The human body is designed for free and easy movement!

Posture – 'In recent years, ergonomists have tried to define postures that minimise unnecessary static work and reduce the forces acting on the body. We could greatly reduce our risk of injury if we stuck to these principles:

129

> **Risk-reducing ergonomic principles**
>
> 1. Work activities should allow you to adopt several different healthy and safe postures.
>
> 2. Where muscular force has to be exerted, the largest appropriate muscle groups should be used.
>
> 3. Activities should be done with the joints at about mid-point of their range of movement. This applies primarily to the head, trunk, and upper limbs (85).

To put this into practice you need to be skilled at observing how you use your own body – your joints and muscles – and readily able to adapt to a healthier style of moving and sitting. It is not easy to do this on your own. The methods outlined in the next section may provide a solution for you.

41. Complementary therapies

This section provides a taster of some helpful methods and principles – there are a range of others. Many who have seriously taken up the practice of one or more of these techniques have minimised or overcome their RSI, improved their pain relief management and enhanced their lifestyle.

a. The Alexander Technique

The Alexander Technique teaches good use of your total self. It enables you to unlearn unhealthy and harmful habits, which have developed over years. Contributing factors to these negative habits include poor seating, long hours of awkward static posture, reacting too quickly without thought, and the excessive tightening of muscles and joints. The unnecessary cumulative tensions that result are often at the root of many ailments, including RSI.

The Alexander Technique 'is a method of releasing unwanted muscular tension throughout your body' (86). It can teach you new ways of carrying out everyday activities like sitting, standing and moving, that will put less strain on your muscles, bones and joints. It pays attention to *active* posture, breathing, balance and co-ordination. It encourages thought before action and thus helps you inhibit your habitual response to stimulus.

The Alexander Technique centres attention on the vital head, neck and back relationship. Your head (weighing roughly 4–6 kgs in an adult) balances at the top of your S-shaped spine, the anchor point for the muscles attaching your arms and legs, as well as the origin of the nerves to your limbs. 'If we lose the optimal length of the spine all our body functions are compromised' (87). When our head-neck-back relationship is used naturally, it provides the anti gravity mechanism we need for good movement and health.

At work, you will find that no matter how good your chair and workstation setup, it is possible to slouch, or putting this more strongly – collapse. When collapsing becomes habitual it may cause physical damage to your body functions, including the blood and nerve supply to your arms, hands and fingers. Because you are used to the way you are, you almost certainly need help to recognise and change your bad habits.

Many RSI sufferers have received enormous benefit from the Alexander Technique, in understanding their total self. They learn to prevent themselves from doing what they have always done, and so go against (bad) habit in order to bring about change and improvement. For real progress a long-term commitment to applying the principle is necessary. This will involve a number of lessons – individual or group sessions. Once you begin to understand the principles, you can apply them to daily life activities – anywhere and at any time without the need of specialist equipment.

'The effectiveness of the Alexander Technique is well documented and is the subject of several scientific studies. It is increasingly recommended by doctors and many medical insurance companies will pay for lessons, if these are recommended by a consultant' (87).

b. Bowen Technique

There are thousands of references to Bowen Technique on the Internet. These notes have been adapted from Bowen Information at (88). The Bowen Technique affects the body primarily through the nervous and the bioenergetic systems, to bring it into a state of balance.

The Bowen Technique is a healing, hands-on therapy that is a simple and powerful technique to help relieve all kinds of pain. It is so gentle that it can be used on anyone, from newborn infants to the elderly. It is based on the work of Tom Bowen in the 1950's.

The practitioner uses thumbs and fingers to gently move muscles and connective tissues. In between each set of moves, the practitioner leaves the room. These pauses and the gentleness of the treatment are what make Bowen unique. It offers rapid, long-lasting relief from pain and discomfort. Most conditions respond within 2–3 treatments. Many RSI suffers have experienced pain relief through Bowen.

While it can help speed up recovery time, the Bowen Technique is not meant to replace medical treatment. However, due to its high rate of success, more members of the medical profession are convinced

of its effectiveness and have begun to add the Bowen
Technique to their practices.

How it works
Bowen Technique helps the body remember how to heal
itself. The Bowen moves send neurological impulses to
the brain resulting in immediate responses of muscle
relaxation and pain reduction. The moves create energy
surges. Electrical impulses sent to the nervous system
remind the body to regain normal movement in joints,
muscles and tendons. This helps relieve muscle spasms
and increase blood and lymph flow.

Bowen Technique affects the body primarily through
the nervous and the bioenergetic systems, to bring it into
a state of balance. One example of how it works is
through the *fascia*. The fascia, sheets of connective
tissue, connects everything in the body: muscles, bones,
internal organs and central nervous system. They play a
major role in muscle coordination, flexibility, postural
alignment and overall structural and functional integrity.
Bowen moves free the relationship between the fascia
and the nerve, muscle or tendon being addressed.

While many experience immediate pain relief,
improvement is just as likely to occur over the days
following a Bowen session.

> *The Alexander Technique and
> the Bowen Technique are
> considered by many to be
> therapies that particularly
> complement each other.*

c. Pilates

The Pilates method is a set of principles and corrective exercises using specialist equipment, which works the whole body in balance. It is a complete fitness method. It combines awareness of the spine and proper breathing and strength, with flexibility training.

As part of rehabilitation programmes Pilates can help resolve the postural problems associated with RSI.

Pilates is normally taught in small groups in a specialist studio. One-to-one lessons can be arranged. To absorb the basic principles takes several months and to maintain the benefits regular practice is essential.

You can find out more by doing a web search on 'Pilates'. The largest teaching association in the UK is the Body Control Pilates Association (89).

d. Yoga

Yoga literally means the union of body, mind and spirit. The practices of exercise, breathing, relaxation, diet, positive thinking and meditation are necessary to unite these three according to the Sivananda philosophy of yoga. When the combination of these is done properly they have a profound and positive effect.

The East tends to see mind, body, and spirit as not only related but inseparable. In contrast in the West they are more usually treated separately. For example, we turn to a psychiatrist for things of the mind, a doctor for our bodies and to religion for our spirits, whereas in the East it is impossible to focus on disease without bearing in mind the state of the mind and the spirit.

Many different types of yoga classes are available in health clubs, gyms, complementary therapy clinics, education establishments etc.

Yoga is sometimes recommended by pain management clinics.

RSI sufferers have usually arrived at this state partly through long periods of sitting in a static position. Through Yoga, the body can be taught to relax and become supple. It can be therapeutic for RSI suffers but could take quite some time for benefits to be obvious.

e. Self care – stretches with Hellerwork

Sharon J Butler, who in 1991 suffered carpal tunnel syndrome, devised this self-help method of very gentle stretching, to prevent and relieve RSI. The information below has been extracted from her book which details numerous stretches, and highlights the benefits of appropriate gentle stretching (24).

Hellerwork is a technique used to restore the body to its normal state of alignment by the stretching and manipulation of connective tissue known as fascia. It can be used for the prevention of RSI and its relief.

Connective tissue is found everywhere in the body and includes blood, bone, tendons and ligaments. It holds the body together joining every part to every other part.

135

Connective tissue also acts as a transmitter and is the reason why the strain of an original injury appears as pain elsewhere.

Fascia, sheets of connective tissue, are involved in the contraction of muscles and their release or lengthening. They are part of the natural protection system – one of the body's best defences against injury. An unusual property of fascia is that it is capable of changing chemically, becoming sticky or dense when they are subjected to stress or injury. When the body is injured through accident or surgery the fascia act quickly to form scar tissue.

Gravity also impacts on the fascia. With good posture natural body alignment is supported by gravity. With poor posture gravity pulls down on whatever is out of alignment, such as a forward head, slumped shoulders, or a curved back. Such imbalance leads to pinched nerves, herniated discs, and joints that do not move efficiently. Some of the fascia becomes tough and fibrous; others become sticky causing muscles next to each other to stick together. Movement is more difficult and a cycle of deterioration sets in making us feel old before time.

The human body is designed for movement and under normal conditions the repetitive nature of ordinary movement, like walking, causes no problem. Rather movement helps the fascia to be loose and fluid. But when the body is subjected to repetitive movements at the same time as being subjected to strain from injury or gravitational forces, the fascia will tighten up or become sticky. A resulting problem is that the fascia cannot return to their good and healthy state without some form of intervention. Stretching is an efficient way of restoring the fascia to their non-binding state.

The method
Gentle stretching can help restore full function and
comfort to painful hands, arms, neck and shoulder.
The Stretch Point is the key to achieving success
through the programme.

The Stretch Point is the very beginning or first hint of a
stretch. If you hold your position when you first feel
this it slowly develops then fades away. You can tell
when you are stretching softly enough if the stretching
sensation disappears completely after 10-15 seconds –
the Release.

Numerous well-illustrated exercises accompanied by
charts to help you choose which exercises are most
suited to your specific problem areas. You develop
your own routine of exercises that you do at points
throughout the day.

42. Trends, costs and legal issues

a. The increasing frequency of RSI

Reports from various countries show that RSI is a global problem fast approaching epidemic proportions.

Some examples:

In the USA

❑ The National Institute of Safety and Health (NIOSH) reports a dramatic growth in the incidence of RSI amongst computer users and also that the elements of injury are probably embedded in normal work habits (90)

❑ Dr. Alan Hedge (director of ergonomic research at Cornell University, New York) agrees, and adds that the increase is pretty much down to the use of the computer, keyboard and mouse. He says it seems that the technical revolution has outpaced human evolution. We are not biologically equipped to perform thousands of repetitive motions an hour (41)

❑ Dr Abner Bevin, Director of the Hand Rehabilitation Centre, University of North Carolina, says the early signs of RSI must be taken as a warning that something needs to change. Because the effects of RSI are cumulative, an analysis of work habits and some change is mandatory. Employment-related medical conditions affecting the upper limbs are of increasing concern around the world. Work-Related Upper Limb Disorders are significant contemporary occupational health problems, estimated to affect many millions of workers around the world annually (41)

In the UK

❑ On BBC News Health website the Pain of RSI is discussed. It points out that RSI sufferers are the victims of technological progress whose use of computers has given them RSI. Many sufferers have an uphill task of convincing their employers their pain is for real (91)

In The Netherlands

❑ RSI seems to be affecting increasing numbers of Dutch employees. Research indicates that in 1999 nearly 30% of the workforce experienced RSI complaints (92)

139

In Australia

❑ RSI is a very common injury among workers in Australia today, affecting computer professionals, hairdressers, butchers, assembly-workers, painters and others (93).

b. Costs

Financial costs to organisations and to nations due to RSI are huge (see Chapter 1). For example, in the UK:

❑ The cost to the UK industry were estimated in 1999 as between £5 billion and £20 billion annually (94)

❑ Dealing with the impact of RSI conditions accounts for between 0.5% and 2% of the gross national income (94)

❑ One large employer found that the average cost of retiring an employee on medical grounds was £40,000 (94)

❑ The highest payment made to an RSI sufferer was £250,000 to a bank worker (95)

❑ RSI results in up to 4.2 million working days being lost in Britain each year (95) .

In addition:

❑ There is the loss as talent and expertise wane when people have to take time off work, or give up altogether

❑ Costs to individuals in terms of pain, discouragement, and job loss are mounting

□   UK Trade Union Committee (TUC) research
      reveals that RSI is second on the list of the
      Top Ten work place hazards in the UK (96).

c.   Wake-up call for employers

Health and Safety experts say a successful RSI claim by
a former Guardian newspaper freelancer should be a
'wake-up call' for employers. Case study 9 outlines this
situation which was propelled into the spotlight in June
2006.

Case Study 9   Guardian pays RSI claim

In two and a half years working nights for the (UK) Guardian Newspaper Andrea worked almost exclusively with a mouse and at speed. On average she worked nine hours a night with few or no breaks. She developed pain in her right elbow and in May 2002 was diagnosed with RSI by her GP. The National Union of Journalists report that requests for a workplace assessment were ignored and that by March 2003, pain stopped her from working.

Nine months later Andrea returned to work on the paper's website. According to her legal representatives, she was refused physiotherapy by the Guardian's Human Resources Department. RSI worsened till she could no longer work.

Discussion and Outcome

- *The Guardian, in refusing to follow basic health and safety procedures, failed in its duty of care.*

- *The Guardian made no admission of liability saying it takes the welfare of its entire staff extremely seriously.*

- ***In June 2006*** *The Guardian paid Andrea £37,500 damages to settle an RSI claim made by her.*

Main sources: (97) and (98)

d.   Reluctance to recognise RSI

In spite of the increase globally in RSI, there remains a hardcore of health professionals who refuse to recognise it as more than another psychosomatic disorder. The problem is also political. Doctors and some government health agencies are reticent to recognise and diagnose a condition that can lead to extensive, and sometimes disputed, claims against employers (41).

Recently musculoskeletal disorders affecting the upper limb have received considerable attention, following financial claims for damages from employees considered to have developed RSI. In this field, increasingly influenced by legal proceedings, important differences of opinion still exist (99).

e. Judgements on RSI claims

Results of research sponsored by the UK Health and Safety Executive on court judgements on personal injury claims for RSI (called WRULD in this instance), in England and Wales, are reported in (99) and on the Web (100). These sites provide a summary of each case that has been verified against the transcript of the Judgement.

Summary of reported cases of court judgements on WRULD, March 1973 to May 2001 (28 years)

Period	Time-span in Years	Number of cases	Number attributed to mouse and/or keyboard	Cases stating keyboard or mouse as the cause, as a percentage of total number of cases in the period
1973-1991	18	70	2	3%
1991-1996	5	72	16	22%
1997-May01	4.25	109	41	38%

This provides a relatively small sample but does fuel the fire of evidence on the increase of RSI due to the use of modern technology like computer keyboard and mouse.

Observations

The dramatic rise in the number of personal injury claims is increasingly ascribed to the use of the keyboard and/or the mouse. The mouse is the worst culprit.

The story is repeated in other countries. For example, in the USA, NIOSH estimates that in less than 10 years, an increase from 18 to 65 percent of all workplace maladies are down and that now accounts for half of all workers' compensation claims (99). This begs the question: 'What will happen to the workforce by the end of this decade, the next, and the next?'

Those responsible for the health and safety of others, take note! Your prime resource is people – people who, like you, live under the escalating and relentless pace of change, accelerated by the microchip revolution. Increasing demands and pressures can adversely affect individuals and society in general.

Employers should understand the causes of RSI, and ensure that everyone in their workforce using computers etc has a workstation assessment. Modifications needed, should speedily be made to their working area.

Before it is too late

*and we are lumbered with an intractable problem,
affecting ever more people, and costing billions,
serious nationwide programmes on prevention
must be put in place, so all people will know*

How to avoid RSI

---

f.   The benefits of prevention

In the USA research reveals that for every dollar invested in an RSI Prevention Programme in an office environment there is a return of 17.80 dollars (94).

Organisations that have a strategy to improve workplace ergonomics have found loss of work time due to musculoskeletal disorders is three times less likely to occur (94).

A success story

Some 40,000 people are employed worldwide by one of the largest international corporations, which is also the second-largest integrated energy company in the United States. Chevron Texaco (renamed in 2005 as Chevron Corporation) takes the health and safety of its employees extremely seriously. In their view every injury is preventable and their safety goal is zero incidents. An outline of the action the company took on discovering the extent of RSI amongst their employees is summarised in Case Study 10.

Case Study 10   The way to go

In 1999, Chevron Texaco found that computer-related RSI accounted for 40% of their workplace injuries worldwide, making them the most common injuries in the company. By 2003, this had dropped to 25%. How? They took action.

In 2001 at vast expense Chevron Texaco reviewed and hence upgraded all IT facilities based on ergonomic principles. When it came to choosing new computers seemingly simple things like mouse clicking, got a lot of scrutiny by their team of health, environment and safety professionals. The company pursued the path of raising RSI awareness and prevention. This RSI Prevention Plan was extended to the whole company.

Improvements include employees being given break software, WorkPace (39). This suggests taking rest breaks, in intervals that can be customized by the individual, and offers demonstrated stretching exercises, etc. Speech recognition is also offered.

The success of the prevention plan, based on early detection and education, is obvious.

Comment – An effective business decision

- *I have been told that not only did Chevron Texaco recoup all expenses involved in a relatively short period through increased productivity, but the workforce are happier, and more effective.*

- ***High praise*** *- Consultant, Shea Dismukes, who has spent 8 years working with multinational companies on ergonomic issues, says: 'Chevron Texaco has the highest level of commitment to RSI prevention I've seen.'*

Source: (101), (102), (103)

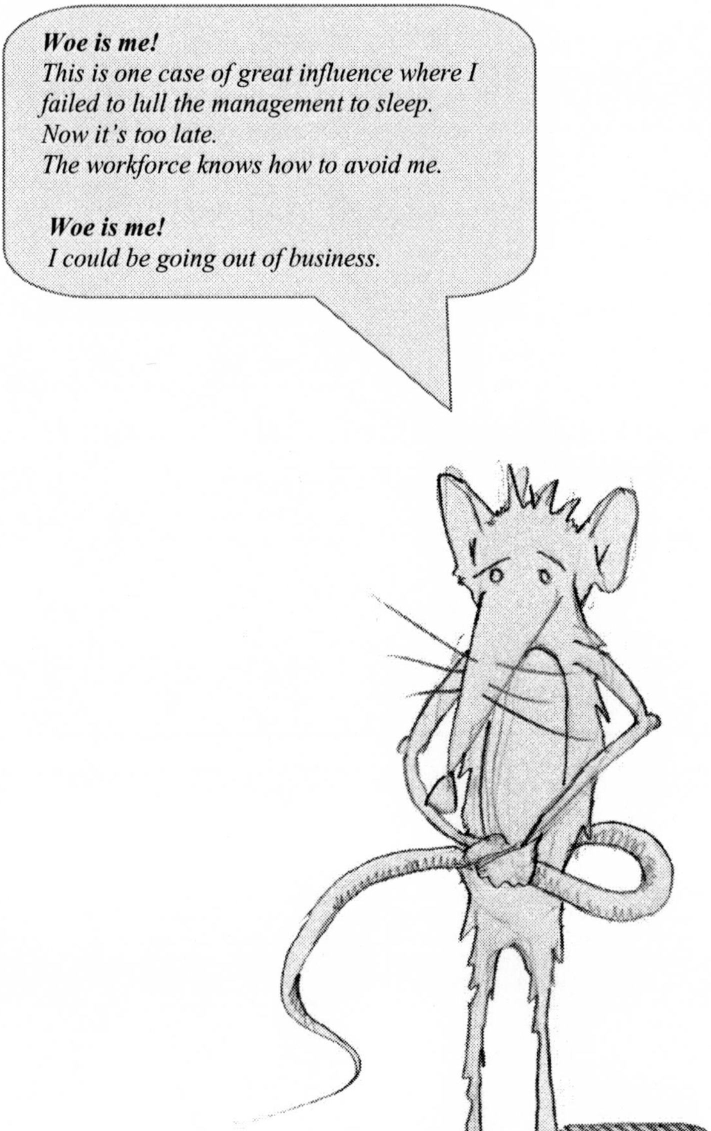
Woe is me!
This is one case of great influence where I failed to lull the management to sleep.
Now it's too late.
The workforce knows how to avoid me.
Woe is me!
I could be going out of business.

F. Tailpiece

As I write these last pages, the wings of my mind fly to a day some seven years ago when I first felt, and ignored, twinges in my wrists and lower arms. I had no idea how continuing to work, in spite of the increasing pains, would quickly force me to STOP and have such long term consequences.

Inwardly I panicked the morning I woke up and found that my body seemed to end at my wrists. My hands had no feeling or strength. With time RSI affected hands, wrists, arms, shoulders and neck. Basic routines like brushing my hair and getting dressed were painful. I could not cut up my food or carry anything, and for two years I could not drive. My children found it hard to understand why I did not want to hold hands.

The first step towards improvement was convincing my employers of the seriousness of the problem. I was diagnosed with Diffuse RSI and advised to take time off work and rest. All this I did, read widely on the subject, and became the default local RSI advisor. This was not enough. After a four-year struggle I (reluctantly) quit my job. Yet this turned out to the best thing I could have done. Away from pressures of demands, deadlines and compulsory computer use I have steadily improved.

Now I work from home and I am determined to help others avoid this debilitating pitfall – hence this book! Writing it has been a challenge but not as big as the challenge 'to practise what I preach'!

PS

TAKE GOOD CARE!
You don't want
short term gain
to be cancelled out by
long term pain!

G. References and further reading

Some references are annotated and the date when an Internet site was last accessed included. **Note:** *Contact details may have changed as firms move on, so check these out.*

1. **Understanding and Treating RSI (Pg. 15)**
   Dr Paul MacLoughlin, The Chelsea Press, 2005
   ISBN 0-9549158-0-1

2. **MIT's RSI Information Page**
   http://web.mit.edu/atic/www/disabilities/rsi/ (Internet 19/07/06)
   This site provided the inspiration for the 'Infamous mouse!'
   throughout this book. It has a section on 'The Workstation
   Setup'. The website is a model of integration providing
   information and links to resources throughout MIT and
   beyond.

3. **Health and Safety Executive, (HSE)**
   www.hse.gov.uk   (Internet 19/07/06)
   Rose Court, 2 Southwark Bridge, London SE1 9HS
   Tel 08701 545500;   Fax 02920 859260
   The HSE is the statutory body responsible for ensuring safety
   at the workplace and hence responsible for ensuring employers
   comply with the 'Display Screen Equipment Regulations' and
   has a legal requirement to implement the principles of
   prevention and protection.

A   INTRODUCTION

4. **TUC Health and Safety**
   www.tuc.org.uk/h_and_s/tuc-4494-f0.cfm   (Internet 19/07/06)
   RSI checklist will spot jobs at risk – one in fifty workers have
   RSI. This briefing points out that "RSI affects millions of people
   around the world, and half a million every year in Britain
   alone. It is entirely preventable and easily curable if caught
   early."

5. **Personneltoday.Com**
   www.personneltoday.com/Articles/2004/11/26/26918/Stress%
   2c+RSI+and+back+strains+are+top+three+health+hazards+in+
   UK.htm   (Internet 19/07/06)
   Stress, RSI and back strains are the top three health hazards in
   the UK workplace.

6. **TUC Health and Safety**
   www.tuc.org.uk/h_and_s/tuc-9059-f0.cfm   (Internet 19/07/06)
   Stress, RSI and back strains are getting worse for UK workers.

7. **Microsoft's Healthy Computing Guide**
    www.microsoft.com/hardware/hcg/hcg_launch.aspx
    (Internet 19/07/06)

8. **The (former) RSI Association**
    www.rsi.org.uk/index.asp   (Internet 19/07/06)
    *On the website of the former RSI Association (now hosted by
    Keytools; see 9 below) there is a comprehensive range of
    information on RSI – causes, treatments, research findings,
    legal issues etc.*

9. **Keytools**
    www.keytools.com   (Internet 19/07/06)
    *Keytools Ltd is a commercial organisation established in 1989
    in the UK with the objective of: "Providing effective special
    needs access equipment for computer users of all ages in
    education, leisure, work, therapy and communication".
    Keytools aims to make IT easier and is certainly helpful.*

10. **International RSI Awareness Day (2003)**
    www.ctdrn.org/rsiday/   (Internet 19/07/06)

11. **Understanding and Treating RSI** (Pg. 3)
    Dr Paul MacLoughlin, The Chelsea Press, 2005
    ISBN 0-9549158-0-1

12. **Dragon Naturally Speaking**
    www.nuance.com/   (Internet 19/07/06)
    *One of the most widely acclaimed speech recognition systems.
    It lets you talk to your computer instead of typing. Competing
    systems include the IBM Via Voice series. Search the net on
    'Dragon Naturally Speaking' to find where to purchase.*

B. FREQUENTLY ASKED QUESTIONS ON RSI

13. **Treatment survey conducted amongst Australian RSI
    sufferers**
    ACT RSI Support Group Inc, P.O. Box 717, Mawson,
    ACT 2607
    RSI Association Newsletter, Spring 2000, Pg. 8

14. **Health at work for computer operators**
    Working Life Research and Development News,
    Newsletter of the National Institute for Working Life
    S-171 84 Solna, Sweden, Tel +46-730 91 00
    RSI Association Newsletter Spring 2000, Pg. 4

15. **Static muscular load, an increasing hazard in modern information technology**Scandinavian Journal of Work Environment and Health, 28(4): 211-213 (Editorial)

16. ℱ **Repetitive Strain Injuries: What You Absolutely Need to Know**
http://web.mit.edu/atic/www/disabilities/rsi/RSIBrochure2004.pdf   (Internet 19/07/06)

17. **Understanding and Treating RSI** (Pg. 74)
Dr Paul MacLoughlin, The Chelsea Press, 2005
ISBN 0-9549158-0-1

18. **Body Action Campaign**
www.just.dial.pipex.com/bacindex.htm   (Internet 19/07/06)
21 Nutwell Street, London SW17 9RS,
Tel 02075-580-0984
The Body Action Campaign seek to raise awareness of the need to protect schoolchildren from RSI by training teachers. (Note – this site is currently being updated/extended, with changes due to go live in August 2006).

19. **Access to Work**
www.jobcentreplus.gov.uk   (Internet 19/07/06)
In UK – check this site if your disability or condition affects your work. Access to Work applies to any paid part time or full time work – permanent or temporary. Help is available including financial support for special equipment or for alterations to your premises. There are leaflets available from Job Centre Plus at the Dept. of Work and Pensions – 'Work Path Programmes', such as:
'Access to Work information for disabled people' and
'Access to Work information for employers'.

20. **Changing Career**
Repetitive Strain Injury Quarterly (RSIQ), Issue 2: June-August 2003, Pg. 7
This is based on the RSIA fact sheet 'Changing Careers and Retraining' available free on the website:
www.rsi.org.uk/changing_careers_retraining.pdf
                                        (Internet 19/07/06)

21. **Professional success and personal well-being**
Repetitive Strain Injury Quarterly (RSIQ), Issue 1: March – May 2003, Pg. 6

22. **Dr. Pascarelli's Complete Guide to Repetitive Strain Injury** (Pg. 88)
Emil Pascarelli, John Wiley & Sons Inc., 2004
ISBN 0-471-38843-2

23. **The British Pain Society**
www.britishpainsociety.org/index.html (Internet 19/07/06)
The largest multidisciplinary, professional organisation in the field of pain within the UK. Membership: medical pain specialists, nurses, physiotherapists, scientists, psychologists, occupational therapists and other professionals actively engaged in the diagnosis and treatment of pain.
People with persistent pain may be able to attend a specialist Pain Clinic for assessment and possible pain management, together with advice on living a fuller life in spite of pain. Get in touch if your pain is persistent and dire.

24. **Conquering Carpal Tunnel Syndrome and other Repetitive Strain Injuries**
Sharon J. Butler, New Harbinger Publications, 1996
ISBN 1-57224-039-3
Gentle exercises to resolve strain and tension in any part of the upper body – well explained and guided. Sharon Butler also has a helpful website:
www.selfcare4rsi.com (Internet 19/07/06)
This excellent self care program is based on the Hellerwork stretching method. It is devoted to helping you recover from RSI – comprehensive information about the following RSIs is included: Carpal Tunnel Syndrome, Tendonitis, Forearm Pain, Tennis Elbow, Neck and Shoulder Pain, and more. If you suspect you have one of these injuries, you will find the information on symptoms, anatomy and self care techniques helpful.

25. **St Thomas' Hospital, London, Pain Management Unit**
www.inputpainunit.org/ (Internet 19/07/06)

26. **It's Not the Carpal Tunnel Syndrome!**
RSI Theory and Therapy for Computer Professionals
Suparna Damany, MSPT & Jack Bellis
ISBN 0-9655109-9-9
Advice on treating RSI injuries (Pg. 187f)
Link to Pain Management (Pg. 38)
(Site temp unavail?) www.RSIProgram.com
(Internet 19/07/06)
Damany, an experienced physical therapist of more than 15 years standing, and co-author Bellis, a long time computer user and recovering patient, focus on computer-related RSI and non-surgical treatment and prevention. Damany works exclusively on RSI patients in private practice in Allentown, Pennsylvania, USA. Through treatments at this clinic many who have given up hope of restored health have been healed, and in the most difficult cases RSI has become manageable.

27. **Where is God when it hurts?**
Philip Yancey, Marshall Pickering, 1998 (Pg. 20)
ISBN 0 551 03164 6
See also Philip Yancey books:
www3.zondervan.com/features/authors/yanceyp/books.htm
(Internet 19/07/06)

28. **Coping successfully with RSI** (Chapter 8)
Maggie Black & Penny Gray, Sheldon Press, 1999
ISBN 0-85969-811-4

29. **Dr N G Kostopoulos**
Holistic Health Centre
Ch. Lada 73, Kifissia, ATHENS
GREECE 145 62

30. **Understanding and Treating RSI** (Chapter 3)
Dr Paul MacLoughlin, The Chelsea Press, 2005
ISBN 0-9549158-0-1

31. **Living with RSI and Overuse Injury**
RSI and Overuse Injury Association of the ACT Inc, Canberra,
Australia
www.rsi.org.au   (Internet 19/07/06)
Phone (02) 6262 5011; Fax (02) 6249 6700
email: rsicanberra@hotmail.com
*The Australian RSI association publication "Living with
RSI/OOS" has a section in the appendix on RSI Friendly
Recipes.*

32. **Bookchair**
www.bookchair.com   (Internet 19/07/06)
*A special reading chair styled as a small wooden deck chair,
designed to prop up a book or magazine on the table.*

33. **The Trigger Point Therapy Workbook**
Your Self-help Guide for Pain Relief
Clair Davies with Amber Davies, New Harbinger Publications
Inc., 2004
ISBN 1-57224-375-9

34. e-stretch
www.e-stretch.net   (Internet 19/07/06)
*Programme produced by Hand Health Unlimited – set up in
1988 and dedicated to helping you take the best care of your
hands. All products are designed to give you increased
strength, coordination, and dexterity in your hands and fingers
and decrease the occurrence of injury, stress, and fatigue.*

35. **RSIGuard**
www.rsiguard.com   (Internet 19/07/06)
*This user-friendly ergonomic intervention software is used by
hundreds of organizations. It has brilliant approval by leading
Ergonomists and Health & Safety Professionals. Studies show
that RSIGuard benefits both the individuals and organisations
that use it. Employers providing RSIGuard for their staff
benefit from increased productivity.*
*RSIGuard includes **BreakTimer** which models strain and tells
you when to take a break. These rest break reminders are timed
based on how hard you actually work at the computer.
Stretches are demonstrates during breaks. **Microbreaks** give
you time to briefly relax, regain awareness of your posture and
work patterns, and maintain awareness of how your body feels.
Ergonomic reminder messages keep you aware of how you are
working at the computer. The **Autoclick** clicks as you hover
the mouse pointer over what you want – alleviating clicking
strain, and more.*
*In the UK, purchase from Keytools (9) who give advice before
you buy as well as providing RSIGuard for a free trial period.*

36. **Fearfully and Wonderfully Made** (adapted from page 163)
Philip Yancey and Dr. Paul Brand, Zondervan, 1987
ISBN 0-310-5451

37. **Chequers Software**
www.cheqsoft.com/break.html   (Internet 19/07/06)
*Break Reminder is a program to help prevent RSI and to assist
in the healing process if these conditions already exist. It
reminds you to take a break – available FREE for personal and
non-profit use.*

38. **WorkPace**
www.workpace.com/rsi.html   (Internet 19/07/06)
*A software package 'for prevention and RSI rehabilitation'. A
trial version can be downloaded.*

39. **ScreamSaver**
www.infinn.com/infopack.html   (Internet 19/07/06)
Protect yourself from computer related injuries (RSI, eye strain, back pain, etc) with ScreamSaver.

40. **Understanding and Treating RSI** (Pg.144-146)
Dr Paul MacLoughlin, The Chelsea Press, 2005
ISBN 0-9549158-0-1

41. **RSI: What can really help**
RSI Association Newsletter, Spring 2000, Pg. 11-12

42. **Posturite UK Ltd (Head Office)**
www.posturite.co.uk   (Internet 19/07/06)
Broad product range, and services geared towards the treatment and prevention of musculoskeletal disorders. Product booklet available on request.

43. **It's Not the Carpal Tunnel Syndrome!**
RSI Theory and Therapy for Computer Professionals
'Advice on treating RSI injuries' (Chapter 8)
Suparna Damany, MSPT & Jack Bellis
ISBN 0-9655109-9-9
www.RSIProgram.com (Site temporarily unavailable)
        (Internet 01/08/06)
This chapter on understanding anatomy sheds light on how the body works and hence how to avoid or beat RSI.

44. **Writing my best seller led to injury**
Repetitive Strain Injury Quarterly (RSIQ), Issue 3: September – November 2003, Pg. 1

45. **ActiveClick**
www.ActiveClick.com   (Internet 19/07/06)
ActiveClick automatically clicks, drags and makes you stretch to help prevent RSI.

46. **Microsoft Mouse and Keyboard products**
www.microsoft.com/hardware/mouseandkeyboard/productlist.
aspx?type=Keyboard   (Internet 19/07/06)

47. **Maltron Keyboards**
www.maltron.com   (Internet 19/07/06)

48. **Osmond – Ergonomic Workplace Solutions**
www.ergonomics.co.uk   (Internet 19/07/06)

49. **Targus – Making your mobile life easier**
www.targus.com/emea   (Internet 19/07/06)

50. **AnimaX International ASA**
www.animax.no   (Internet 19/07/06)
Oslo, Norway: Phone +47 22 66 0500; Fax 47 22 66 0501

Provides a step-by-step illustrated guide to ergonomic computer use.

51. **Squeaky Mouse to tackle RSI**
BBC News Wednesday 10 May 2000, 14:20 GMT 15:20 UK
http://news.bbc.co.uk/hi/english/sci/tech/newsid_742000/7424
46.stm   (Internet 19/07/06)

52. **The MouseTrapper**
www.mousetrapper.co.uk   (Internet 19/07/06)
Relieves typing stress. Free trial available for order at the website above.

53. **Understanding and Treating RSI** (Pg. 114-117)
Dr Paul MacLoughlin, The Chelsea Press, 2005
ISBN 0-9549158-0-1

54. **Ergonomics of using a mouse or other non-keyboard input device**
Research Report 045, HSE Books, UK
ISBN 0-7176-2162-6
Order, or download from the following web address:
www.hse.gov.uk/research/rrpdf/rr045.pdf   (Internet 19/07/06)

55. **Keyboard shortcuts**
www.support.microsoft.com/default.aspx?scid=kb;en-
us;q126449#appliesto   (Internet 19/07/06)
The shortcuts given here are for Windows and are a subset of those on the Microsoft website. Used regularly these can reduce the mouse-strain on your hands.

56. **Understanding and Treating RSI** (Pg. 151-156)
Dr Paul MacLoughlin, The Chelsea Press, 2005
ISBN 0-9549158-0-1

57. **Latest Text Messaging SMS News**
Release 27 September 2005
www.text.it/mediacentre/default.asp?intPageId=848
                          (Internet 28/10/05; no longer archived)

58. **Latest Text Messaging SMS News**
Release 23 August 2005
www.text.it/mediacentre/default.asp?intPageId=847
                          (Internet 28/10/05; no longer archived)

160

Text.it - *the UK's official guide to text messaging is the place to look to keep up to date on Texting:* www.text.it/home.cfm.
See for example **Volume of texts during the World Cup 06** *posted*

> *Figures released by the Mobile Data Association (MDA) show that 112 million messages were sent on average per day throughout June, with the total monthly figure topping 3.37 billion. In the first six months of 2006 over 18 billion person-to-person text messages were sent in the UK, well on the way to the MDA's annual forecast of 36.5 billion.*
>
> *On 15th June and 1st July, when England played Trinidad & Tobago and Portugal 140 million messages were sent. This was equivalent to an average of 6 million messages sent per hour, and is second only to the current daily record of 165 million messages sent on New Year's Day this year.* Internet 08/08/06)

25/07/06

59. **Chartered Society of Physiotherapy (CSP)**
    www.csp.org.uk   (Internet 19/07/06)

60. **Mobile Data Association**
    www.themda.org/Page_Default.asp   (Internet 19/07/06)
    A non-profit service for vendors and users of mobile phones.

C.   CHILDREN BEWARE

61. **Understanding and Treating RSI** (Pg. 17)
    Dr Paul MacLoughlin, The Chelsea Press, 2005
    ISBN 0-9549158-0-1

62. **Shanghai Teenagers Addicted to Computers: Survey**
    www.iwantmedia.com/internet.html   (Internet 20/07/06)

63. **China moves to zap online game addiction**
    Financial Times, Asia-Pacific, August 2005
    www.ft.com/cms/s/89ea206a-13f3-11da-af53-
    00000e2511c8.html   (Internet 20/07/06)

64. **China forced to rethink online gaming limit**
    www.tiscali.co.uk/news/newswire.php/news/reuters/2006/03/2
    2/technology/china-forced-to-rethink-online-gaming-limit-
    ft.html&template=/technology/feeds/story_template.html
                                      (Internet 20/07/06)

65. **Prevention and rehabilitation makes good business sense**
    Repetitive Strain Injury Quarterly (RSIQ), Issue 2: June –
    August 2003, Pg. 1

66. **Understanding and Treating RSI** (Pg. 18)
    Dr Paul MacLoughlin, The Chelsea Press, 2005
    ISBN 0-9549158-0-1

67. **Dr. Pascarelli's Complete Guide to Repetitive Strain Injury**
    (Pg. 160)
    Emil Pascarelli, John Wiley & Sons Inc., 2004
    ISBN 0-471-38843-2

68. **Health and safety issues relating to the use of computers in
    schools**
    http://Education.otago.ac.nz/NZLNet/safety/health_and_safety.
    html   (Internet 20/07/06)
    A helpful New Zealand website for students and teachers.

69. **The RSI Generation**
    Article from The Daily Mail (UK), 12 April 2000

70. **Understanding and Treating RSI** (Pg. 121-124)
    Dr Paul MacLoughlin, The Chelsea Press, 2005
    ISBN 0-9549158-0-1

E.   DIGGING DEEPER

71. **Repetitive Strain Injury in the Member States of the
    European Union: the results of an information request**
    http://agency.osha.eu.int/publications/reports/303/index.htm
                                            (Internet 20/07/06)
    *The findings of a new European Agency for Safety & Health at
    Work Report – based on a survey questionnaire distributed in
    1999.*

72. **Repetitive Strain Injury Source Book** (Pg. 37 -38)
    Sandra Peddie with Craig H Rosenberg, M. D. Lowell House,
    USA, 1997
    ISBN 1-56565-791-8

73. **Medical explanation of pain syndromes – Diffuse RSI
    (WMSDs)**
    Dr Bill Turner, consultant occupational physician,
    Christchurch, New Zealand
    http://repetitive-stress-injury.workpace.com/WP
    :MOREHOWCANRSIBECOMEACHRON
    *The WorkPace site has useful information on medical research
    into RSI, prevention methods, recovery, computer use tips etc.:*
    www.workpace.com/rsi.HTML   (Internet 20/07/06)

74. **A Vascular Basis for Repetitive Strain Injury**
    M.H. Prichard, N. Pugh, I Wright and M. Brownlee

162

Department of Rheumatology, Department of Medical Physics
and Department of Cardiology, University Hospital of Wales,
Health Park, Cardiff, UK
Rheumatology 38: 366-639 (1999) (Printed in summary form
in the RSI Association Newsletter, Autumn 1999, Pg. 8)
*Concerns the first part of a current research programme into
the diffuse form of RSI.*

75. **Review of Diagnostic Criteria for Work Related Upper
Limb Disorders (WRULD)**
Report for the Health and Safety Executive
Professor Alan J. Silman MSc MD FCRP FFPHM and Jason
Newman BSc
University of Manchester Medical School, February 1996
www.hse.gov.uk/research/misc/silman.pdf (Internet 20/07/06)

76. **Reduced median nerve movement in RSI patients**
Jane Greening, Sean Smart, Rachel Leary, Margaret Hall-
Craggs, Paul O'Higgins, Bruce Lynn
The Lancet 354: 217-218 (July 17, 1999)

77. **Researchers at UCL find physical proof of RSI**
RSI Association Newsletter, Autumn 1999

78. **RSI EXISTS – Study reveals medical evidence for RSI**
Reported in Office Worker, City Centre, Spring 1998, Pg. 4

79. **Scientists trace RSI nerve centre**
Tim Radford Science Editor
The Guardian, Friday July 16, 1999
www.guardian.co.uk/uk_news/story/0,3604,282480,00.html
(Internet 20/07/06)

80. **Medical Multimedia Group**
288 West Main St, Suite D, Missoula, Montana, 59802, USA
www.medicalmultimediagroup.com/index.html
(Internet 20/07/06)
*Illustrations revealing some of the intertwined complexity of
nerves in the arm are available on the following site:*
www.eorthopod.com/eorthopodV2/index.php/fuseaction/topics
.detail/ID/79791a8f7dd9f446b38653cbeab9a955/TopicID/2f08
cb47d2d0f85d66a33fad17b62d34/area/10 (Internet 20/07/06)

81. **Role of Mechanical and psychological factors in the onset of
forearm pain: prospective population based study**
Gary J Macfarlane, Isabelle M Hunt, Alan J Silman
BMJ 321:676 (16 September 2000)
http://bmj.bmjjournals.com/ (Internet 20/07/06)

82. **BODY – An Amazing Tour of Human Anatomy**
(with free CD)
Robert Winston, Dorling Kindersley Publishers, 2005

163

ISBN 1-4053-1042-1
This book provides an incredible tour of the human body;
pictures in 3D developed from actual body scans, and a CD
that reveal astonishing things going on under your skin that
make you tick. The sections on 'Hand and Wrist', 'Shoulder',
'Arm and Elbow' and 'Head' show the complexity and
dexterity of these body parts that most of us take for granted as
we spend hours and hours using modern technology.

83. **Understanding and Treating RSI** (Pg. 81)
Dr Paul MacLoughlin, The Chelsea Press, 2005
ISBN 0-9549158-0-1

84. **Ergonomics 4 Schools**
www.ergonomics4schools.com/   (Internet 20/07/06)
This is a most helpful and interesting website.

85. **Ergonomics.org – Posture, movement and ergonomics**
(Including The Alexander Technique)
www.ergonomics.org   (Internet 20/07/06)

86. **The Alexander Technique Manual**
A step-by-step guide to improve breathing, posture and
well being (Pg. 10)
Richard Brennan, Little, Brown and Company, 1996
ISBN 0-316-87497-3

87. **About the Alexander Technique**
www.ati-net.com/ati-alex.php   (Internet 20/07/06)
This site includes several book recommendations.

88. **Bowen Technique**
www.boweninfo.com/   (Internet 20/07/06)

89. **Body Control Pilates Association**
6 Langley Street, London, WC2H 9JA
Tel (020) 7379 3734
www.bodycontrol.co.uk/contact.html   (Internet 20/07/06)

90. **National Institute of Safety and Health (NIOSH) – USA**
www.cdc.gov/niosh/homepage.html   (Internet 20/07/06)

91. **The Pain of RSI (BBC News: Health. March 2002)**
http://news.bbc.co.uk/1/hi/health/1844459.stmBBC
          (Internet 20/07/06)
This is an evidence-rich site with numerous examples of
personal RSI accounts. It has advice to employers on how to
tackle Repetitive Strain Injury.

92. **RSI threatens to become leading work-related illness**
The Netherlands, European industrial relations observatory online (eironline)

www.eiro.eurofound.eu.int/2000/04/inbrief/nl0004186n.html
(Internet 20/07/06)

93. **Australia – RSI – Home Page**
www.rsi.org.au/ (Internet 20/07/06)
*RSI is a very common injury among workers in Australia
today, affecting computer professionals, hairdressers,
butchers, assembly-workers, painters and others.*

94. **RSI Facts and Figures, RSI Association**
www.rsi.org.uk/Facts_&_Figures.pdf (Internet 20/07/06)

95. **BBC NEWS / Health / RSI**
http://search.bbc.co.uk/cgi-
bin/search/results.pl?scope=all&edition=d&q=RSI
(Internet 20/07/06)
*This is a rich site pointing to much useful information on RSI –
and will keep you up to date with RSI happenings!*

96. **TUC calls for new EU law**
RSI Association Newsletter, December 2002, Pg. 6

97. **Companies warned after RSI payout over mouse use**
Tom Espiner, ZDNet UK, June 08, 2006, 11:10 BST
http://news.zdnet.co.uk/business/legal/0,39020651,39273857,0
0.htm (Internet 20/07/06)

98. **'Disgraceful' Guardian pays out £37k to RSI sub editor**
Dominic Ponsford, 24 May 2006
www.pressgazette.co.uk/article/240506/disgraceful_guardian_
pays_out_37k_to_rsi_sub (Internet 20/07/06)

99. **International RSI epidemic**
Trade Magazine – Health and Safety at work, April 2000

100. **How the Courts are interpreting HSE guidance and health
and safety regulations. An exploratory study of Court
Judgements in personal injury claims for WRULDs**
Brian Pearce, Research School in Ergonomics and Human
Factors, Loughborough University, prepared for the Health and
Safety Executive, 2002
ISBN 0-7176-2536-2
This document is available online at:
www.hse.gov.uk/research/rrpdf/rr010.pdf (Internet 20/07/06)
Case summaries are available at:
www.humanetechnology.co.uk/wruld/intro2.php
(Internet 20/07/06)

101. **Chevron Texaco, the global magazine**
June/July 2002, Volume 1, Number 2
www.chevron.com/news/publications/jun02/docs/cvx_jun02.p
df (Internet 20/07/06)

165

102. **Chevron 2005 Corporate Responsibility Report**
www.chevron.com/cr_report/2005/priorities_progress_plans/he
alth_safety/   (Internet 20/07/06)

103. **Chevron Texaco Company profile**
http://www.chevron.com/about/company_profile/
                                                (Internet 20/07/06)

FURTHER READING

104. **Kid-kind computing**
Taking safety steps for computer-mad children
Franklin Tessler, MacWorld, November 2000

105. **Computers in schools are putting elementary
schoolchildren at risk for posture problems**
Cornell computers and ergonomics, USA
www.news.cornell.edu/releases/Feb99/kids.computers.ssl.html
                                                (Internet 20/07/06)

106. **Computers 'could disable children'**
BBC correspondent Christine Stewart, BBC News Website,
Sunday, 26 November 2000
http://news.bbc.co.uk/1/low/health/1041677.stm
                                                (Internet 20/07/06)

107. **Children Risk Developing Repetitive Strain Injury**
RSI Association newsletter, Winter 2000, Pg. 3

108. **Researchers studying ergonomics for kids**
CNN Sci-Tech story page, April 21, 1997
www.cnn.com/TECH/9704/21/kidernomics/index.html
                                                (Internet 20/07/06)

109. **RSI: everything you need to know about this scourge of the
office**
Angela Green, Daily Mail, Tuesday January 9, 2001
Includes a discussion on children by Bunny Martin.

110. **Computerfit: Staying Healthy in a Computer-Based
Workforce**
Randall Helm, Lifelong Health Systems, 1997
ISBN 0-9682652-0-0
www.computerfit.com
(Internet 09/03/01; site not avail. on 24/07/06)

111. **Repetitive Strain Injury: A Computer User's Guide**
Pascarelli and Quiller, Wylie, 1994
Good on prevention.

112. **Australian RSI site**
www.rsi.org.au/links.html   (Internet 20/07/06)
Links on this site are worth exploring.

113. **OPERA Software**
www.opera.com/   (Internet 20/07/06)
*Opera is a web browser which allows the use of a keyboard
rather than a mouse for virtually everything.*

114. **Cumulative Trauma Disorder Networks**
www.ctdrn.org/rsi-support/   (Internet 20/07/06)
Loads of RSI information.

115. **SOREHAND Support Network**
www.ucsf.edu/sorehand/   (Internet 20/07/06)
*US-based and with a high volume of messages. Hunt through
the archives for useful postings.*

116. **Computing Out-Loud**
www.out-loud.com/
    (Internet 20/07/06)
*Written by Susan Fulton, this is an excellent
site on voice recognition. It includes user
reports on programs and assorted gadgets,
useful macros and links to the main
software manufacturers' sites.*

117. **Understanding the Alexander Technique**
Joan Diamond
First Stone Publishing
4/5, The Marina, Harbour Road,
Lydney, Gloucestershire, GL15 5ET, UK.
*The number of good, helpful books on The Alexander
Technique is growing. The merit of this compact well
illustrated booklet (affordable at only £1.99) is that gives an
easy to digest insight into this therapy – how it was invented;
how it works; what it can do for you*

118. **Understanding the Bowen Technique**
Joan Diamond
First Stone Publishing
4/5, The Marina, Harbour Road,
Lydney, Gloucestershire, GL15 5ET, UK.
*Published in association with the Bowen Therapy Academy of
Australia and the Bowen Association of the UK. This booklet is
in the same style as the 'The Alexander Technique' (Ref 117).*

119. **RSI Action**
www.rsiaction.org.uk   (Internet 08/08/06)
RSI Action is the new (2006) national RSI charity
RSI Action, PO Box 173,
Royston, Hertfordshire, SG8 0WT, UK

120. **Computer-Related Repetitive Strain Injury**
http://eeshop.unl.edu/rsi.html   (Internet 20/07/06)
RSI sufferer Paul Marxhausen has developed this useful
website to help others. It contains good basic advice on
prevention, and points to other websites and books on RSI.

A personal tribute:

Mark, thank you.

Your site was of great help in my early
days as an RSI sufferer – and I still
check it out.

Tonia

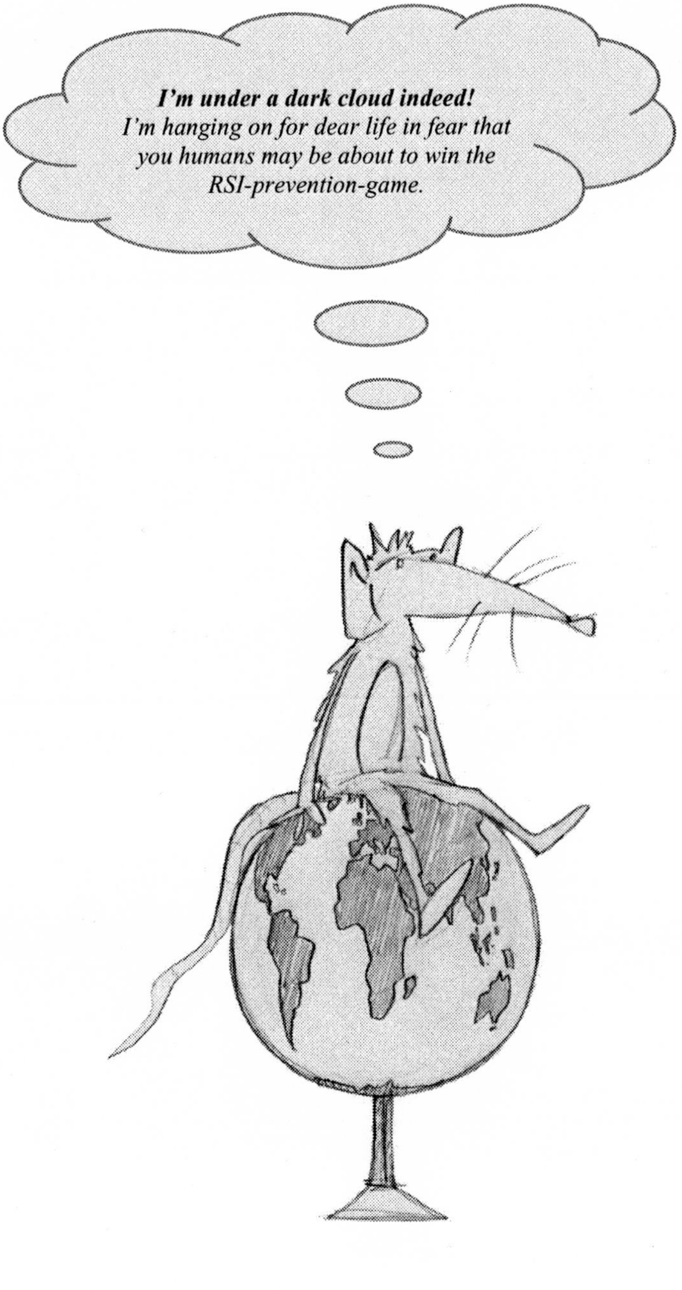
I'm under a dark cloud indeed!
I'm hanging on for dear life in fear that you humans may be about to win the RSI-prevention-game.

H. Index

172

176

178

180

I. Acronyms

BBC	British Broadcasting Association
CSP	Chartered Society of Physiotherapists
CTD	Cumulative Trauma Disorders
CTS	Carpal Tunnel Syndrome
HSE	Health and Safety Executive
MDA	Mobile Data Association
MIT	Massachusetts Institute of Technology
MSD	Musculo Skeletal Disorder
MSI	Musculo-skeletal Injury
NIOSH	The National Institute of Safety and Health
NSAP	Non-Specific foreArm Pain
NSPS	Non Specific Pain Syndrome
OOS	Occupational Overuse Syndrome
PCT	Primary Care Trust
RSI	Repetitive Strain Injury
TUC	Trade Union Committee
UCL	University College London
ULD	Upper Limb Disorder
WMSD	Work-related MusculoSkeletal Disorder
WRULD	Work-Related Upper Limb Disorder

J. About the Author and Illustrator

Tonia Cope Bowley

A South African farm girl, Tonia gained a B.Sc. degree at Natal University and a Teaching Diploma at Cape Town (UCT). For the next six years she taught senior school mathematics in South Africa before spending a year on a working holiday in the Arctic Circle, Norway.

From 1973–2001 Tonia was on the staff at Oxford University where she was involved in various research and teaching projects, all with a strong IT element. Her book on BASIC, published in 1981, was a best seller. For several years she developed and ran an Image Processing Centre. At that time she carried out research on the usefulness of Satellite Remote Sensing for Third World Urban planning with Durban as the case study.

In 2001 Tonia, happy in her work, reluctantly accepted the University's offer of medical retirement due to prolonged chronic repetitive strain injury. However this has proved liberating and led not only to her virtual recovery from RSI but has given her more valued time with her family, space to develop her creative skills as a writer (this book being an example), and gardener, and her work in the charity sector.

Last but not least, in 1988, Tonia and her husband Stephen launched The Thembisa Trust, a registered charity supporting disadvantaged people at the grassroots in 'The Beloved Country' – South Africa.
www.thembisatrust.org

William Harding

After completing a foundation course at the University of the West of England in Bristol, Will gained BA (Hons.) degree in Animation at Edinburgh College of Art. While in Edinburgh he was commissioned to produce a flipbook by Edinburgh University that was used as the official 'Student Survival Guide' in 2001.

In 2002 he became a freelance web designer, illustrator and model maker. He worked as an assistant sculptor for Bad Dog Design. There he helped to sculpt the stage piece Baffta head for the award ceremony in 2003. For the last three years he has been a model maker at Aardman Animation working on their feature film 'The Curse of the Wear Rabbit', short films and adverts.

Recently, with freelance illustrator, Gwen Millward, Will has set up Gingerbeast – a web design company.
Gingerbeast.co.uk

K. Summary

How to avoid RSI

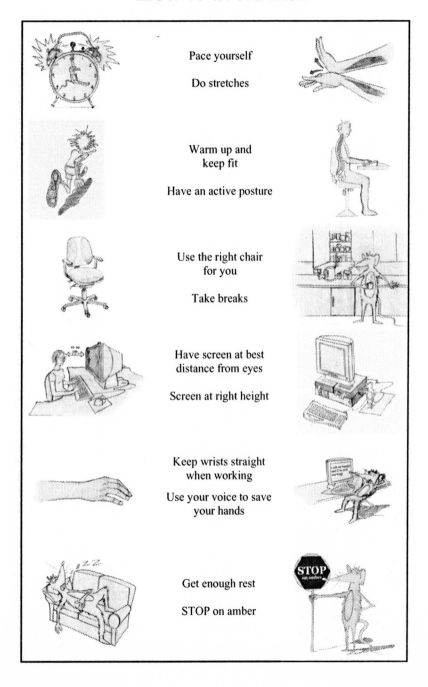

Pace yourself

Do stretches

Warm up and
keep fit

Have an active posture

Use the right chair
for you

Take breaks

Have screen at best
distance from eyes

Screen at right height

Keep wrists straight
when working

Use your voice to save
your hands

Get enough rest

STOP on amber